S0-AZB-604

ELISSA MONTANTI is the founder of the Global Medical Relief Fund, a one-woman organization dedicated to helping children injured in war zones. She lives in Staten Island, New York.

JENNIFER HAUPT is a journalist who has written for *O, The Oprah Magazine; Psychology Today;* and *Ladies' Home Journal,* among others. She is currently working on a debut novel.

---

## Praise for *I'll Stand by You*

"Elissa Montanti is the saint of Staten Island." —*People*

"Elissa Montanti, with little money and no experience in humanitarian aid, has changed the fortunes of more than one hundred crippled children, one child at a time."
—Scott Pelley, *60 Minutes*

"An intriguing journey begins with tragic loss in the seemingly safe suburbs of Staten Island, and stretches across the rugged terrain of lawless hinterlands of war-torn Bosnia to find a new life of unexpected adventure and ultimate redemption. This very personal story proves that one person can make a powerful difference in the lives of thousands."
—Deborah Rodriguez, author of the *New York Times* bestseller
*Kabul Beauty School*

WITHDRAWN FROM

"The author's spirits are as changed in this straightforward and sweet narrative as the lives of those she helped—and she finds hope, happiness, and love along her difficult but rewarding journey." —*Publishers Weekly*

"A moving testament to the will and single-mindedness of one woman determined to help those in need." —*Kirkus Reviews*

"This book shows us what can be done." —*Library Journal*

"The story is an inspirational one that should make people feel empathetic toward kids who, through no fault of their own, wind up victims of war-zone violence." —*Booklist*

"In *I'll Stand by You*, Elissa Montanti grips you from start to finish. She pours her heart and soul into getting these children the proper medical care as they become a part of her global family. Shriners Hospitals for Children is proud to play a role in providing the care that many of these families can't afford, nor can these children receive in their homeland."
—Peter F. Armstrong, MD, vice president of Medical Affairs, chief medical officer Shriners Hospitals for Children

# I'LL STAND BY YOU

*One Woman's Mission to*
*Heal the Children of the World*

# ELISSA MONTANTI

*with Jennifer Haupt*

A PLUME BOOK

PLUME
Published by the Penguin Group
Penguin Group (USA) Inc., 375 Hudson Street
New York, New York 10014, USA

USA / Canada / UK / Ireland / Australia / New Zealand / India / South Africa / China
Penguin Books Ltd, Registered Offices: 80 Strand, London WC2R 0RL, England
For more information about the Penguin Group visit penguin.com

First published in the United States of America by Dutton, a member of Penguin Group (USA)
Inc., 2012
First Plume Printing 2013

Copyright © Elissa Montanti, 2012
All rights reserved. No part of this product may be reproduced, scanned, or distributed in any
printed or electronic form without permission. Please do not participate in or encourage piracy
of copyrighted materials in violation of the author's rights. Purchase only authorized editions.

All insert photos courtesy of Elissa Montanti except for page 2, top and middle, courtesy of
Kenan Malkic; and page 8, middle, courtesy of Anthony D'Antuono.

"Let's Do a Miracle" lyrics by Elissa Montanti and Pam D'Ambrosio
"Chimes in the Wind" lyrics by Elissa Montanti; music by Anthony D'Antuono
"Sand Castles" lyrics by Elissa Montanti; music by James Dawson and Seth David Walker
"Back Together Again" lyrics by by Elissa Montanti, James Dawson, and Seth David Walker;
music by James Dawson and Seth David Walker

 REGISTERED TRADEMARK—MARCA REGISTRADA

THE LIBRARY OF CONGRESS HAS CATALOGUED THE DUTTON EDITION AS FOLLOWS:
Montanti, Elissa.
    I'll stand by you : one woman's mission to heal the children of the world / by Elissa Montanti
with Jennifer Haupt.
        p. cm.
    ISBN 978-0-525-95295-4 (hc.)
    ISBN 978-0-14-219689-2 (pbk.)
1. Montanti, Elissa. 2. Global Medical Relief Fund. 3. Child Health services—United States. 4.
World health. 5. Children and war. 6. War relief. 7. War wounds—Treatment. 8. Prosthesis. 9.
Biomedical technicians—New York (State)—New York—Biography. I. Haupt, Jennifer. II. Title.
    RJ101.M645 2012
    362.198'920092—dc22        2012005232
    [B]

Printed in the United States of America
10  9  8  7  6  5  4  3  2  1

Set in Adobe Berkley Book

While the author has made every effort to provide accurate telephone numbers, Internet
addresses, and other contact information at the time of publication, neither the publisher nor the
author assumes any responsibility for errors or for changes that occur after publication. Further,
the publisher does not have any control over and does not assume any responsibility for author
or third-party Web sites or their content.

Some names have been changed to protect the privacy of the individuals involved.

Penguin is committed to publishing works of quality and integrity.
In that spirit, we are proud to offer this book to our readers;
however, the story, the experiences, and the words
are the author's alone.

# DEDICATIONS

*To my father*: A World War II veteran who served in the Aleutian Islands and South Pacific campaigns, who was present at Tokyo Bay at the signing of the surrender of the Japanese Empire on the USS *Missouri*. With a heart as big as the world that he has traveled and his mind as open as the sea that he has sailed, he knows no distinction in color or creed, only a great and deep empathy for humanity.

In the face of adversity and the darkest of night, he will find humor and will see tomorrow's light. These values, ethics, and integrity are those of my hero, Louis J. Montanti. I love you, Daddy.

*To Kenan*: You are this story. Because of you we have helped heal the world's children, one child at a time. You are their purest hope and their inspiration. You are the pulse and heartbeat of GMRF. I feel your joy and your pain, as I know you share mine. You are my "little big miracle." You are my salvation and I am so proud to call you "son." *Volim te puno.*

*To my mother, Rita*: As Grandma would always say, "God never closes a door without opening a window." I feel your hand waving each time a gentle breeze passes through the window of my walk-in closet "office." I know you're with me every step on the path that I have chosen. I miss you more than all of the stars in the sky. Until we meet again, I miss you and love you, Mommy.

# CONTENTS

❦

# INTRODUCTION: HOW COULD I NOT?

❦

❧ "Why do you do this?" People ask me that question all the time.

It's been fourteen years since I launched Global Medical Relief Fund, a little charity I run out of a former walk-in closet in my Staten Island townhouse. Fourteen years of answering emails from Bosnia, Iraq, and Africa in the middle of the night. Fourteen years of spending most of my paycheck to bring one more child here for a new leg or arm—a new life. Eleven years since I left my ordinary nine-to-five job as a medical assistant in order to do anything and everything but the ordinary. During this time I've given up sleep, any hope of a vacation, and my marriage. (Not to mention a place to hang my clothes!)

I've given up a lot, so I understand the question. But look what I've gained.

———

When fifteen-year-old Kenan Malkic arrived at John F. Kennedy Airport with his mother in November 1997, the first thing he said to me after hello was, "I like your shoes." He was used to looking down to avoid the stares of pity and wonder. More than anything, he just wanted to be an ordinary kid again. Normal.

After five years of battling near-debilitating depression and panic attacks, I knew some of what this child was feeling. I knew it had been a long, hard journey for him to get here.

In September 1994, three years earlier, Kenan had been playing soccer with some friends in a designated safe zone: a protected valley hidden away from the hills surrounding the small town of Maglaj, Bosnia, where snipers were hiding. After two years, war had become a way of life. During the quiet periods—like now—people came up from their protected basements to run errands or just get some fresh air. It was a brief chance for children to be kids again.

Kenan, a tall, wiry boy built for playing goalie, lunged to catch the ball soaring toward him but missed. He didn't think twice about running to retrieve it from a patch of tall grass at the edge of the field. As he reached for the ball, he felt the force first in his mouth, then his chest, as he was knocked to the ground. Lying facedown in the dirt, shocked and numb, the taste of blood and gunpowder in his mouth, he heard shouting, screaming.

When Kenan got to the hospital, the doctors in the emergency room were shouting as people were ripping off his soccer jersey and jeans: "Find some anesthesia! Cut up some sheets if there's no gauze—we need something to stop the bleeding."

*Don't let me die, just don't let me die,* Kenan prayed as he sunk into unconsciousness. Meanwhile, his mother was in the waiting room, desperately praying for her only child. Doctors told her that they weren't sure if he would ever wake up again.

When Kenan did wake up a few days later, his eyes crusted shut by the blast, his body scarred and encased in pain, he could feel that he had lost both of his arms and a leg. "There is no future," he told his mother flatly. "Put me back to sleep again."

It didn't take long for me to find out that not only was I helping Kenan by taking him into my Staten Island home for four months while he was fitted for state-of-the-art prosthetic limbs he couldn't get in his own country, but he was also helping me. This has been the case with each of the more than 150 children from around the globe I've taken into my home and my life since Kenan's first trip here.

There's a story, "The Starfish Thrower," that goes something like this: A man is walking along the beach and notices a woman going back and forth, again and again, between the water and the sand. As he gets closer, he stops and laughs: this crazy woman is actually picking up the starfish stranded on the beach, one by one, and tossing them back into the ocean. "Lady, look, there are thousands of miles of beach and God only knows how many of those little creatures," he says, shaking his head. "One person can't possibly make much of a difference in saving them."

The woman stoops down to pick up a glistening purple starfish, dusts it off, and gently casts it back into the waves, then turns to the man and smiles. "It sure made a difference to that one!"

I am that crazy woman. And the injured children I bring to the United States for new limbs and new smiles are like the starfish. They come to me mostly through emails from soldiers serving in Iraq, reporters covering a tsunami in Indonesia or an earthquake in Pakistan, doctors and humanitarian aid workers who can't ignore a desperate plea from a mother in Haiti or Libya. All of these people are searching for the same thing I found when I saw a photo of Kenan lying in his hospital bed after the land mine accident that left him missing three limbs. Incredibly, I was certain that I could help him even though I was going through the darkest period of my own life. The people who bring these kids to me are also looking to gently pick up one beautiful, shining starfish and toss it back into the ocean, where it can begin life again.

Sometimes it truly takes a global village to help one child. I found fifteen-year-old Ali Ameer in a hot, crowded hospital room in Basra, Iraq, not long after the shock-and-awe bombing of Baghdad in March 2003. When he waved his bandaged arm in the air and smiled at me from across the room, it was like a big, wonderful magnet. I sat on his bed, showing him my photo album with photos of Kenan playing basketball, cooking breakfast, and typing on the computer with—and without— his prosthetic leg and two prosthetic arms. A doctor told me that Ali's hand had been blown off when, while helping his father sell gasoline at the marketplace, the boy picked up a shiny object: a land mine. Ali pointed to a photo of Kenan drinking from a cup with his new hands, then he held up his own arm that ended in a stump, pointing to himself with his other hand. The look in his eyes was so hopeful. How could I say no?

It took a year of untangling red tape in Iraq and the United States; doctors in Kuwait, Basra, and Philadelphia; and a seven-year-old girl in Virginia who rallied her Girl Scout troop and second grade class to write letters to their congressman (among others) to bring Ali here for a prosthetic hand. And Kenan, who was living with me and going to college by this time, was with him every step of the way—from doctor visits, to showing him how to manipulate the robotic limb, to playing soccer and basketball. Ali opened the door for dozens of other injured children from Iraq to come to Staten Island to heal, and helping him made me stronger too. If I could force open all of the doors trying to shut in my face over the year it took to secure permission to bring him here, I could battle my own demons, which were still floating to the surface. I couldn't do it for myself, but I could do it for the growing number of kids who needed my help.

Kenan has been living with me now for more than fourteen years, and Ali has visited three times since he's outgrown his original prosthetic hand. All of the children who have come here—multiple times as they grow and need new prosthetics—have become part of my global family. The love I have for these kids and they have for each other is bigger than anything I could have ever imagined. It is surely bigger than my walk-in closet in Staten Island. It is as big as the world.

So, why do I do this?

How can I not?

# ❧ I'LL STAND BY YOU ❧

## CHAPTER ONE

# From Staten Island to Bosnia

*Staten Island, New York, early 1960s*

Family has always been important to me, and that term cast a broad net in the mostly Italian neighborhood on the east shore end of Staten Island where I grew up. It was the early sixties, before the highway ramp to the Verrazano-Narrows Bridge connecting the island with Brooklyn and the rest of the world was built. Progress was not a friend to Major Avenue once that ramp was built. The century-old chestnut trees that had lined the sidewalks were cut down to widen the road. The woods where we built forts out of branches and hunted for black-berries and other treasures was paved over. The twinkling lights I saw from my bedroom window were no longer a billion stars in the pitch-dark night, but the distant glare of car head-lights moving across the gray constellation of steel and wire. I remember being seven years old, standing on the sidewalk, watching with terrified awe—along with my older sister, Rita Lu, and a crowd of our neighbors—as a yellow crane heaved a wrecking ball back and forth, back and forth. With mighty swings this black metal ball knocked down the walls of my friend Bobby's house, up the street from mine on the corner of

Lily Pond Avenue. Today, there's still a big dip in the road where there used to be an actual pond filled with beautiful yellow lilies at the edge of the woods before the bridge was built.

"What if the ball goes back too far and smashes our house?" I squeaked, squeezing my hands tightly over my ears to muffle the noise of wood beams splintering and brick walls crashing to the ground. I knew the ball couldn't really knock down our house, but Bobby's rec room was like my second home.

My sister was staring at the wrecking ball, so angry I could feel her shaking next to me. "These guys don't know what the heck they're doing," she said.

"Should we go get our stuff from our room?" I asked. I really just wanted her to tell me that everything was going to be okay.

I like to remember the neighborhood during the magic years before that, though, when nobody locked their doors and every groan of the screen door hinges held the promise of a friend coming through with a new 45 record or asking me to play red light/green light or a game of jacks. The night air rang with the symphony of crickets, roller skates clicking down the sidewalk, and the jingling bells on Nicky Sugar's ice cream truck coming down the street—instead of cars roaring on the freeway leading to Brooklyn.

Everyone in the old neighborhood used to meet on the stoop of my family's home at 71 Major Avenue in the warm summer evenings. This was the same house that my grandmother's brother Dante built for my grandparents in the forties, and where my mother's parents still lived with us. My mom's brother Louie and his family were just across a connecting backyard. Our houses were so close that once my cousin Mimi and I spent an entire Saturday morning tying string together and trying to talk to each other through tin cans. When the cans didn't work, we pressed our lips against the window screens and screamed: "Hello? Hello, can you hear me now?"

In fact, our entire block was like one big, mostly Italian family: Bobby up the street, Frankie next door, Sallie from across the street, and I were like the Little Rascals. (I was Darla, the only girl.) My sister, Rita Lu, who's four years older than me, and her friends were the revered "big kids" who got first dibs on Kool-Aid and cookies when we all congregated in our kitchen after elementary school. Everyone hung out in the "clubhouse"—which is what we called our garage, complete with an old fridge, a Formica table and chairs, and our names as well as those of our favorite bands carved in the ceiling beams. Along one wall was a table with an old victrola that my parents gave us when they bought their first hi-fi console (stereos weren't even invented yet) in 1963. And there were probably a dozen boxes filled with 45 records that Sallie's father periodically traded out from the jukebox at his penny arcade, where we would sometimes go on Saturday afternoons, spending our ten cent allowances on Now and Later candies and Tootsie Pops (three for a penny), watching the big kids play the latest pinball games or electronic baseball.

Summer was the best time of year: Frank Sinatra and Dean Martin wafted through the screen door of our house while my mother—Mommy, as Rita Lu and I would always call her, even after we were grown—and her friends sat on that stoop and drank tall glasses of lemonade with lots of ice. Rita Montanti was beautiful inside and out, with a Donna Reed hairdo and soft, inviting features. Her big heart showed in her warm brown eyes and sincere smile. That's probably why so many women in the neighborhood confided in her, considering her their best friend.

While the moms were chatting on the stoop, we'd be belting out the Duprees' "Have You Heard" or the Platters' "Smoke Gets in Your Eyes" in the clubhouse. Or we'd be practicing one of the many shows we liked to put on, charging two cents per audience member. We'd splurge on egg creams at Sam's Corner with our spoils. Rita Lu and her friends did this great routine where they blacked out their teeth and did a phony toothpaste commercial, and I sang "It was an itsy bitsy teenie weenie yellow polka-dot bikini" in front of paper waves. When I was six years old, Mommy made Roaring Twenties outfits for all of us: feather boas, knee-length flapper skirts with a double tier of glittery string sewn to the edges, and fishnet stockings for the girls, and black vests, bow ties, and fake mustaches for the boys. For two weeks, we practiced the Charleston. When the time came for our big show, Mommy and Daddy were right there in the front row, clapping and laughing louder than anyone. At least that's how I'll always remember it.

My mother loved all kinds of music, and she had a strong, sweet voice. It was comforting to hear her sing along to Broadway show tunes or the smooth crooners of the day—Dean Martin, Perry Como, Connie Francis—while she vacuumed or helped Grandma Nellie with dinner. Sometimes she moved the Singer sewing machine from the basement into the dining room to listen to music while making me a new skirt and matching headband or Rita Lu a dress. Mommy wrote her own poems, sometimes leaving one under my pillow for a birthday or "just because it's an especially perfect day." She even made brown bag lunches fun: hard-boiled eggs with smiley faces drawn on the shells.

My father preferred opera, Mario Lanza and Ezio Pinza, to Dean Martin. He had a global view before that phrase was coined. While Mommy couldn't imagine anywhere she'd rather be than 71 Major Avenue—except maybe a weekend at Wildwood Beach on the Jersey Shore—Daddy was a wanderer. He was an officer in the Merchant Marine and loved the promise of adventure on the open sea. His job took him to Europe, Asia, and Indonesia for weeks at a time. He'd come back with a big duffel bag full of exotic souvenirs: dolls, spices, fireworks for the Fourth of July. It was always a party when my father came home.

When I was fourteen, Daddy returned from a month-long trip to Greece, and he literally came waltzing into the house, snapping his fingers gaily and wearing a white Greek sailor's cap and a blue tunic shirt with gold braiding. My sister and I rushed him with our usual tackle of hugs and kisses, reaching for the duffel bag slung over his shoulder that typically held our gifts. He put up his hand like a stop sign. "I'm afraid that you're under the mistaken impression that I am some very fortunate man who goes by 'Daddy,'" he said in a foreign accent I can only assume was supposed to be Greek.

"Our mistake," Rita Lu said, laughing. "We shoulda known by the fancy shirt."

"Just call me Zorba," Daddy said, putting his hands out to his sides, bending his knees deeply and snapping his fingers. It was early 1968, three years after *Zorba the Greek* came out in the theaters, and this was Lou Montanti's rendition of Anthony Quinn's *sirtaki*, a traditional Greek dance.

"Well, I don't care who you are," Mommy said, planting a big kiss on her husband's lips, tilting his hat to one side. "I'm just glad to see you."

Daddy began dancing around our mother, then over to the hi-fi console, where he put on a 45 record he had in his coat pocket. "Oopah!" he said, as "Zorba the Greek" began playing. "All the way from Greece!"

"As long as you're here, instead of our father . . . ," I said, eyeing the bulging duffel bag that Daddy had dropped in the center of the room.

"Age and beauty first," he said, now dancing around the bag. Grandma Nellie and Grandpa Joe were watching us with amused smiles from their respective chairs at either side of the nubbly green couch. Daddy acted like a showman at center stage as he pulled a bottle of ouzo out of the bag and gave it to Grandpa, kissing him on the cheek. Then, he made a huge production of pulling out from the bag colorful gold-threaded scarves for Mommy and Grandma Nellie, Greek sailor dolls for Rita Lu and me, and an assortment of seashells he'd found on the beach.

That night, Grandma Nellie made a big pot of pasta with fresh tomatoes she'd bought that morning from the fruit vendor who drove around Staten Island in an old blue pick-up truck. I kept staring at the seashells my mother had placed in a cut-glass bowl in the middle of the table as a centerpiece. They were mostly broken and dull, but the prisms of glass and the light from the chandelier above made them glisten as if they were still being washed over by ocean waves. "How far is it from Staten Island to Greece?" I asked my father. "Maybe I'll go there someday." I wanted more than anything to dance on the beach like Anthony Quinn did in *Zorba the Greek*, collect seashells, and have an adventure.

"You may as well be asking how far away is the moon," Rita Lu deadpanned, always the pragmatic one. I shrugged. The world was a big place, and I would see it someday. But for now, there was absolutely no place as wonderful as home.

*Maglaj, Bosnia, early 1990s*

Everyone knew each other in the small town of Maglaj, Bosnia, where Kenan Malkic grew up. People looked out for each other; kids ran in and out of their neighbors' unlocked doors. Mothers and grandmothers sat on front stoops and balconies dotted with pots of colorful flowers, trading recipes and stories about their children. The Malkics' neighborhood was kind of like my big extended Italian family on Major Avenue, except nestled in a valley with the silhouette of mountains against the sky instead of Manhattan skyscrapers. And instead of split-level ranch houses, there were mostly apartment buildings that housed about twenty families, with communal gardens where neighbors grew vegetables and flowers. Small farms surrounded the town. In the fall harvest season, Kenan and his friends would dare each other to run into a farmer's field and steal a few ears of corn, then build a bonfire by the side of the road to roast their bounty.

Miralem Malkic was a career military man who had earned

his major's stripes and was stationed in town at a desk job by the time his son was born. Kenan idolized his father, missing him terribly when he went away for three or four days every few months. Some weekends, Miralem would let his son tag along when his unit went to clean up a World War II memorial site in the mountains. Other times, when the soldiers were practicing military exercises—which was more and more frequently after the fall of the Berlin Wall in 1989—he would sit his son down and say, "You need to stay here and take care of your mother. While I'm gone, you're the man of the house. Understand?" The little boy nodded solemnly, promising to do all of his chores and take a bath without arguing.

During the summer, the best day of Kenan's week was Saturday, when he would go fishing with his father in the Bosna River. Aida would pack them a picnic lunch—crackers, meat, cheese, and fruit—that father and son would eat while sitting on the grassy bank just below an old cobblestone and wood footbridge, where the trout liked to hang out in the shade. Miralem was a quiet man with strong Slavic features, casting and recasting his rod, keeping an eye on the water, which was so clear you could sometimes spot the bigger fish. Kenan loved to watch their catch swimming around in a bucket of water while he talked to his father about school and his friends.

Aida, a petite woman with classic beauty—fair skin, light brown eyes, blonde hair, and a full-lipped smile her son inherited—was the social one of Kenan's parents. Kenan knew if he was walking with his mother to the grocery store just a few blocks away, it would be a long journey, with all the stopping to ask how someone's sick mother was or if their baby had cut that new tooth yet. If you asked Kenan, his mother was maybe a little too friendly. She even stopped to talk with the crabby old man who lived in the house just in front of their apartment building, the one who yelled if you went to get a soccer ball that was accidentally kicked into his garden. Everyone hated this guy—except Kenan's mother.

A little more than two years after the Berlin Wall fell, in April 1992, the Orthodox Serbian government of Slobodan Milosevic declared war on Bosnia and Herzegovina, embarking on a campaign to rid the region of Muslims and reclaim the region. Everything changed in Kenan's mostly Muslim town, but it didn't happen overnight. There would be an incident here or there— shots ringing out in the night, or an explosion that blocked a main road. Miralem started putting together neighborhood watch groups for the town entrances and exits, and that's when Kenan first realized that something was going on. He stopped asking to come along when his father had to leave town, which was happening more and more often now.

One warm spring night Kenan and Aida were sitting out on their balcony, admiring the stars against a cloudless dark sky. "That's weird," Kenan said, pointing to a bright tunnel of light shining from above. "I wonder what's up there?"

"It's nothing, I'm sure," Aida said. But then two more streams of light appeared. The triangle was like a target, right over the Bosnian Army headquarters where Miralem worked.

"Come inside," Aida said in a hollow voice that gave Kenan a chill. "Don't worry, your father's coming home soon."

Aida and Kenan sat at the kitchen table, staring out the window at the triangle of bright light for what seemed like hours but was probably only minutes. Then, a loud explosion cracked the quiet night and a cloud of smoke blocked out the beams of light as well as the stars. *Where is he?* Kenan just looked at his mother, unable to form the words. Suddenly, people were running in the hallway, knocking on neighbors' doors.

The Hodzics from next door came over. "Where's Miralem? Why aren't you listening to the news?" Mrs. Hodzic asked, clicking on the small radio on the kitchen counter. Aida was still sitting in a chair, as if frozen. Kenan stood with his arm protectively around his mother's stiff shoulders, hearing his father's strong, calm voice: *While I'm gone, you're the man of the house. Understand?*

Mrs. Hodzic flipped from music to static, eventually landing on the sound of a deep, grave voice. "I repeat, the army headquarters in Maglaj has been hit, wounding dozens of people and killing three top military officials." Kenan felt his mother stiffen as the announcer read the three names. One was his father's.

"This is bullshit," Mr. Hodzic said, turning off the radio. "The Serbs have been releasing false information all day, trying to scare us, playing with our minds."

"Mom?" Kenan asked, his voice high and shaky.

"Don't worry, your father will be home soon," Aida said flatly, picking up the phone, holding it to her ear . . . it was dead.

The next few hours were terrifying as she sat with her son, reassuring him that everything was fine, silently praying her husband would come home. When Miralem walked through the door she began laughing and crying at the same time.

"What happened to you?" he asked, unaware of the radio broadcast.

"You're not dead?" she asked, looking at him as if she couldn't quite believe it.

"No," Miralem said matter-of-factly. "I'm not dead."

"That's good," Aida said, getting up to hug her husband, to feel him solidly in her arms. "You see, Kenan? It was nothing."

But what Kenan could see was that both of his parents were scared. He knew that things would never be the same in his small town. Things would never be the same for him or for his family.

## CHAPTER TWO

# The Wrecking Ball

When I was fifteen, four years after the bridge was completed, our neighborhood was quieter—especially our house. Music has always been such a big and wonderful part of my life, and my family. Not long after my father came back from his trip to Greece, Mommy started playing mostly sad love songs instead of the happy crooners and show tunes she loved. I knew something had to be wrong. The somber melodies seemed to fit a change in her personality; she'd always been so cheerful and energetic. Now her smile was tighter, her eyes not as bright. One night, Rita Lu and I heard sharp voices coming from the kitchen. "Oh dear God, not again," I said.

"Go to sleep, Elissa," my sister whispered, both of us laying in our beds in the dark. "Hopefully, it's nothing."

"Hopefully . . . G'night, Ri." I knew my sister was trying to reassure herself as much as me. And we both knew these recent outbursts of emotions were far from normal for our parents.

A few weeks later, I came home from school to find Mommy sitting on the couch, her black Donna Reed hairdo and coral lips perfect as always, but her features were sallow and drawn. Rita Lu was next to her, already home from her day of classes at the College of Staten Island, where she was in her first year of nursing school. I gave my sister a "what's going on?" look, and she slowly shook her head. "Sit down, Elissa," she said softly.

My mother held us both close to her and let out a long, shaky breath. I waited, holding my own breath, feeling Mommy sit up straighter as if inserting an invisible steel rod in her spine. "Your father's leaving us," she said.

"Is he going out to sea for awhile again?" I asked. But now I was getting a queasy feeling.

"No, not like that," Rita Lu said, trying to spare my mother having to say the words again. "He's going away—for good."

*Divorce.* None of us could say the word. Even the next day when my father came home and tried to explain why he was leaving, he couldn't say that word. "I love you girls, your mother—I love this family," he said, tears streaming down his face.

My worst nightmare had become a reality.

"Then don't leave us. Please, Daddy. People in love, they argue, but that doesn't mean anything." I looked to Rita Lu, but she wouldn't look at me. We were both sobbing, but she had this hard glint in her eyes as she was staring at our father. Her face clouded over with anger as he haltingly explained that he'd gotten involved with another woman. Daddy kept talking, explaining that there were difficult circumstances, he still loved Rita Lu and me. Our mother. When he left with his suitcases, I ran upstairs and curled up on my bed, crying like a baby. My father had always been my hero, and now he suddenly came crashing down off the pedestal. How could he do this? It was unfathomable.

Months later, I would learn that I had a three-year-old sister, and that's why Daddy left to marry another woman. That's what men of honor did in his day. In years to come, I would grow to love my father's new wife, Margot, and learn that life can get complicated and things happen. But at the time, it sounded as if his voice was coming through the same tin can that cousin Mimi and I used to play telephone. I couldn't help but think of that wrecking ball, tearing down Bobby's house many years ago. I felt the weight of it, crashing right into my chest, destroying my safe and happy home.

Shortly after Daddy moved out, Mommy was diagnosed with lymphoma. I often wonder if she knew she was ill, even before Daddy left, and didn't want to tell him how serious it was. She wouldn't want him to stay just because she was sick. And yet he's told me many times that he would have stayed if he had known. The truth is he never stopped loving my mother.

For years, I couldn't shake loose this idea that if I just kept quiet and pretended nothing was wrong, all of the sorrow would just blow over—my father leaving, my mother's illness—and we could somehow go back to being a happy family. Of course, deep down I knew this wasn't true. I remember sitting in my room, cranking up Perry Como's "It's Impossible" or George Harrison's "All Things Must Pass" so that nobody could hear me crying. But when I left that room, I left behind my pain. I remember admonishing my big sister, who wasn't as skilled as I was at hiding emotions, "If you're going to cry, go to your room. But when you walk into the same room as Mommy, make sure you have a smile on your face. She's got enough to worry about without adding you and me to the list."

"You're Mommy's sunshine, sweet petunia," Grandma Nellie would say, as if she was depending on me. I could always make

Mommy laugh, and we'd talk about everything—boys, school, my summer job answering the phone at an insurance company. But never death. "I'll be fine, I know what I have and I'm under a doctor's care," Mommy would say. "There are plenty of people who are sick and don't even know it. But me, I'll be fine." For many years, that was the closest she'd come to admitting she had cancer. So, who was I to complain that I was scared out of my mind? I tried not to even think about how I was feeling; all that was important was making my mother smile.

Mommy wouldn't let anyone take care of her—not even her own mother. She'd come downstairs every morning with her hair fixed and lipstick on, even when her beautiful raven hair started falling out from the chemo and she was too nauseated to eat.

"Let me make breakfast this morning," Grandma Nellie would say, trying to take her daughter's arm to guide her into a chair. "I'll get you a nice cup of coffee, a little sweet and light, just like you like."

"Ma, I'm okay," Mommy would insist, gently pushing Grandma Nellie away, turning on the frying pan. "Eggs or waffles, girls? Elissa, you'd better hurry or you'll be late for school."

Even though our mother was headstrong and independent throughout the eleven years she battled cancer, she cherished the strong group of women who supported her. Every morning at seven thirty sharp Aunt Tessie—who wasn't really my aunt but Mommy's best friend since high school—would call to check in on her, as always, even before Mommy was sick. Tessie and her two sisters, along with Mommy's friend Mildred and Aunt Mezzie, would all take turns bringing Mommy to her chemo and radiology appointments, and one of them was constantly at the house. They laughed and talked, never about anything serious. Certainly never about cancer.

We were basically a household of women after Daddy left: Mommy, Grandma Nellie, Rita Lu, me. (Grandpa Joe spent a lot of time in the cellar, making wine from the cherries that grew on two trees in the backyard and working on his many inventions.) Aunt Mezzie and cousin Mimi were just across the yard. Mezzie was the spitting image of Ethel Mertz—and funny like Ethel too. And Mommy's dear friend Mildred would come in from the city and spend the weekend. When my mother was in remission and strong enough to get out of bed, we'd all get together in our living room—sitting on and around that nubbly green couch covered in crocheted pillows and Grandma Nellie's latest bright knitted afghan. Mezzie would make us each a Brandy Alexander and Grandma Nellie would make her famous *zeppela*—fried dough covered in powdered sugar that just melted on your tongue. We told jokes and listened to music, all of us giggling hysterically over the silliest things. Mildred was a real card: she'd put on Dean Martin's "Everybody Loves Somebody" and change up the words. "Everybody loves some money, sometime," she'd belt out. And I'd get out my goofiest 45s. There was an Italian song by Nicola Paone, complaining that all his wife does all day is talk. "Yakety, yakety, yak," we'd all sing along at the chorus, laughing so hard we were crying. Those times were such a relief; if I could just keep Mommy happy, everything would be okay. And for more than six years, off and on, that seemed to work.

———

Some of the best times I had as a teenager after Mommy became ill were the trips we took together to visit her cousin Rita in

South Jersey. There was this great teen dance club run by the community in a school—they served Cokes and played records in a gymnasium-style room—where Rita's daughter, also named Rita, took me and my friend Barbara one weekend not long after my mother was diagnosed with cancer. I was so excited because it was where the college guys from South Philly sometimes hung out.

"Check out the guy who just walked in, he's dead-on Tom Jones!" my friend Barbara whispered, grabbing my arm as we sat drinking our sodas and trying to look sixteen-year-old cool.

"Definitely college," I said, appraising the well-built guy with smoothed-down curly brown hair. He was wearing khakis, a navy blazer, and a loose striped tie; the top button of his light blue Oxford shirt was unbuttoned. I also noticed we weren't the only ones looking at him. "And definitely way out of our league," I sighed, following Barbara toward the bathroom to make sure our slips weren't showing and our cobalt-blue eye shadow was on thick enough.

"Let's see when we go out if we can catch his eye and get the nerve to smile," I said.

I stayed in the bathroom, flipping my long straight black hair. But when I came out of the bathroom, Tom Jones was standing right in the hallway, aiming a dazzling smile straight at me. It took all of my sixteen-year-old cool not to pass out!

"Well, hello. I'm Alfie," he said, sounding more South Philly than London. That was just fine by me. Up close, he was even more attractive. It wasn't that he was drop-dead gorgeous, but there was just something about him. You could tell he was special, but not in a pretentious way. And the better I got to know Alfie, the truer I found this to be.

"Well, hello yourself," I said, trying to be cool even though I was intoxicated by that smile. "Elissa."

"What's with that accent?" he asked.

"New York," I said. It sounded more impressive than Staten Island—besides, he'd never know. It wasn't like this guy was going to call me.

I felt a little guilty as I danced the stroll arm in arm with my South Philly Tom Jones, seeing how Barbara had pointed him out to me. But only a little. Alfie and I wound up talking and dancing all night. When he asked for my number I hesitated. "You don't want me to call?" he asked.

"No, it's not that. It's just, well, I live on Staten Island, not in the city."

Alfie laughed softly, then gently brushed his lips against mine. It wasn't the most passionate first kiss I've ever had, but it was definitely the most romantic. He charmed me that night we first met, just as he would charm all of the women in my family.

Date me, date my family—that's how both Alfie's family and mine were, old school Italians, all of them. I was sixteen and he was nineteen, so all of our parents were particularly protective of me. Truthfully, everyone knew there was nothing to worry about. During the five years that we dated each other, Alfie and I never did more than kiss. Oh, but what kisses!

I was Mommy's sunshine during the first five years of her illness, but Alfie was the blazing sun that lit up our entire household. "Alfie's coming in a few hours, let's get this place clean!"

Grandma Nellie would command like a drill sergeant. Even when Mommy wasn't feeling well, she always seemed a little better when he showed up at the door on a weekend with a box of pastries from a famous Italian bakery in South Philly.

Alfie usually came with his older brother Sammy and his younger cousin Johnny, and they would go on dates with my friends. We'd all hang out in the living room—where the guys slept when they visited—playing Beatles songs backward and searching for hidden messages until Mommy threatened, with a laugh, to commit hari kari if she heard that song one more time. I'd come downstairs around nine in the morning, and Grandma Nellie—Grandmum, as Alfie called her—would already be serving my boyfriend his breakfast, peppering him with questions. "So how's your mother's garden doing? Those two younger sisters of yours, are they studying hard or just giggling about boys? And how's your father's bad back?" Alfie would answer in between bites of eggs, sausage, toast, and fried potatoes. Grandma Nellie judged a man by three things: his appetite, what his father did for a living, and if he had clean shoes.

During those years, we spent a lot of Sunday dinners at Alfie's house in Philadelphia, which is about a two-hour drive from Staten Island. His family lived in a modest part of town full of row houses, the same neighborhood where *Rocky* was filmed. There must have been twenty people sitting around that dinner table between our two families, eating manicotti and drinking Chianti, talking loud, and laughing louder. Sometimes I'd catch Mommy and Alfie's mother, Adeline, giving each other a knowing glace and then looking at me and Alfie. Everyone thought we were going to get married—including me for awhile. Alfie put me on a pedestal—writing me love letters with quotes from poets or romantic musicals like *West Side Story*. "There's a place for us, somewhere's a place for us . . ."

Alfie bought me gifts even though he didn't have much money—nothing expensive, but impressive nonetheless. Case in point: one time he made a life-size poster of me from a photo to hang in his dorm room. He was the first man who truly loved me, and I just took for granted that's how relationships would always be. The problem, when it came down to it, was that I was young and didn't really know what love was. I adored being with Alfie, but I also wanted to date other guys. When I broke up with Alfie for the first time, to go to my senior prom with a boy I don't even remember, Grandma Nellie was so angry she wouldn't speak to me for days. Worse, though, was when my mother called me into her bedroom and shut the door to have a private talk.

"Elissa, how can you throw away something so rare to find in life?" Mommy said to me. I couldn't help but think she was still asking that question of my father. "You think you'll find someone else to love you like that? Let me tell you, you're going to have a tough time of it."

Alfie and I got back together a few months later, and we dated off and on for most of the years that Mommy was sick. But I never could commit fully to him, which was the big argument that led to each of our break-ups, including the final one. In retrospect, maybe I didn't think I deserved to be loved the way that he loved me—the way that my father had once loved my mother. And she wound up being right: it took me twenty years to find another man I trusted so completely. But for the time being, I was more concerned with the person who had always been number one in my heart: my mother.

———

After high school I took a job as a medical lab assistant at Doctors' Hospital on Staten Island, where Rita Lu worked. I wasn't really sure what I wanted to do with my life—except my music, poetry, and painting, and finding ways to make my mother smile. She was really pleased that I had a good job, but there was definitely a downside. Now, I was right there when Mommy came in to get her blood tests, and I knew how to read the results. Every week was an emotional roller-coaster, waiting to see if her white blood cell count was up and she was well enough for another round of chemotherapy. She couldn't pretend to be feeling better than she was, although I still pretended not to know when things were really bad. There were nights when, instead of going straight home from work, I drove to the beach in my car, sat looking out at the water for hours, and cried until it was out of my system. Sometimes Rita Lu came with me; mostly, though, I went alone.

I was twenty-two and my sister was twenty-six when she decided to go on a year-long road trip by herself to Alaska. Rita Lu had been talking about doing this since high school, and I was inspired that she was actually following her dream. *Maybe*, I thought, *I could do the same*. I signed up for an American literature class at the Staten Island community college because I loved to write.

That summer was the best one I had since my childhood: Mommy was well enough to go to the Jersey Shore with me and Mildred. Alfie and I got back together and we spent the weekends going to outdoor concerts—Iron Butterfly, Eric Clapton, the Beach Boys—or taking long walk-and-talks on the beach. He'd take me to the Philadelphia Museum of Art and run up and down the seventy-two stone steps, just like Rocky Balboa had done. We sat by the fountain, talking, sometimes throwing in pennies to try our luck at making wishes come true. He had just graduated from Penn State with a degree in economics and was interviewing at large corporations on Wall Street and in Philadelphia. He told me his dream of saving money to go to law school, and I shared my dream of applying for art school after a year or two of community college. Both of our futures were looking bright, and it seemed like we might actually have a future together.

Mommy seemed to be doing so well during this time, but what we didn't know was that there was a time bomb ticking away in her stomach. All of the radiation she was undergoing to treat the cancer had created ulcers, but she was so used to the pain that she didn't complain when it became worse. One night I was just getting ready to watch *Butch Cassidy and the Sundance Kid* when my best friend, Frankie, who still lived next door, stopped by. "Hey, how about heading over to grab a pizza at Nunzio's?" he asked.

"Sure, okay," I said, but I had this heavy feeling I couldn't shake, like something wasn't right. I couldn't eat much, and when I came home there was a possum on the front lawn that scared me half to death. He looked up at me, baring his teeth, then ran away. It seemed like a bad omen, and not ten minutes later my mother was doubled over with pain. I called Uncle Louie, who rushed across the backyard to drive us to the hospital. My mother sat next to me in the backseat, still doubled over, while I rubbed her head, trying to soothe her.

I waited six hours with Uncle Louie and Aunt Mezzie while Mommy was in emergency surgery. Aunt Mezzie had called Rita Lu, but she was fogged in at an airport in Alaska for the next two days. That night I kept pacing, praying, "I know Mommy's going to be okay. Please, God, she has to be okay."

"Of course she is," Aunt Mezzie said, eating one chocolate bar after another to soothe herself. I wished with all of my might that Rita Lu's plane would take off soon so she could be by my side.

It turned out that Mommy had a ruptured colon that developed peritonitis, an inflammation of the membrane that covers the abdominal organs and produces a life-threatening bacteria that spreads through the blood and lymph system. Her entire body was in shock, and a perforation had exploded in her intestinal wall. The surgeon who operated on her said it was a miracle that she lived, and she stayed in the hospital for six months, hooked up to a respirator. Luckily, during that time Rita Lu and I both worked in the hospital so we could keep an eye on her, visiting during our breaks. In the evenings we both stayed with Mommy, holding her hand while she slept, or telling her about our day.

When Mommy finally came home she moved into my bedroom, both of us sleeping side by side in the twin beds where Rita Lu and I had slept as kids. I was so scared that she'd wake up in the middle of the night needing pain medicine, a glass of water, or just someone to hold her hand and nobody would be there. Sometimes I'd hear her labored breathing in the dark at night and turn on my bedside lamp to write in my journal, letting my fears take the shape of poetry and song lyrics so that I could stay calm and strong for my mother. Sometimes, while waiting for her medication to kick in and her breathing to ease, I'd just write over and over, "Dear God, please don't take Mommy. She has to live."

I missed my sister so much while she was gone, but I was disappointed that she had to cut her Alaska adventure short because our mother was ill. And she was shocked at the sight of me. During the eight months she'd been away, my face had broken out in terrible acne. As bad as I appeared on the outside, I felt even worse on the inside. The anxiety and fear I was plagued by was exhausting and all consuming; I'd dropped out of community college and I'd all but stopped seeing Alfie. I knew that nobody could help me—not Alfie, not Rita Lu—because what I needed to feel better was impossible: I needed to save my mother.

The only real relief I found during my mother's final years was in my writing and music. After Rita Lu came home, she joined me and Mommy in our room, sleeping in a cot at the foot of our beds so that she could give our mother shots of painkiller and medication during the night. I turned Mommy's bedroom into a music room, complete with my amps and posters of rock stars. I'd escape into that room, often in the middle of the night when I couldn't sleep. I'd turn on my stereo and put on big puffy headphones that blocked out the rest of the world, while I softly sang along with Joan Baez and Joni Mitchell. That was the only place I let myself be free.

## CHAPTER THREE

# When the Music Stopped

❧

During the next few years my mother was in and out of remission—as well as in and out of the hospital—numerous times. Just after Thanksgiving 1978, Mommy checked in for a routine stay, just a few days for a simple blood transfusion. But she developed a cold that her body was too weak to fight off, and it quickly turned into pneumonia. After a week on oxygen, I asked a doctor if she'd be home in time for Christmas. He looked at me like I was nuts: "Honey, she's not coming home at all," he said. That's how I found out my mother was dying.

On December ninth, my sister's thirtieth birthday, we went to the hospital with my mom's two brothers, my father's brother Vincent, and my father to see her. It was clear she was fighting to hang on, weaving in and out of consciousness. "Elissa? Rita Lu?" she'd say, waking up with a start, and we'd squeeze her hand. This went on for hours, my father by her side the whole time.

Toward the late afternoon, she turned to my father and smiled, more coherent than she'd been in days. "Louie," she whispered, gasping to talk despite the oxygen mask on her face. "Remember Arizona? All of those stars at night?"

My father nodded, a faraway dreamy look on his face. "South Mountain Park, of course. You were pregnant with Rita Lu. We were so happy." He leaned closer to my mother, holding both of her hands as tears slid down his face, and gently kissed her cheek. "Rita, those were the happiest days of my life."

Mommy died at 4:10 the next morning; my father was the last person she kissed good-night.

At the funeral I was numb, immersed in a mixture of grief and relief. Finally, the eleven years of suffering she'd been going through were over and she could rest. But I couldn't imagine life without her. I sat at the back of the funeral parlor while everyone stood in line and viewed the casket. Daddy came and sat next to me. "Are you sure you don't want to see her one last time?" he asked.

I shook my head and then placed it on his shoulder. "I want to remember Mommy at her best—surprising me with a snack at night, singing 'Love Me Tender' along with Elvis Presley. Waking me up in the winter to make sure I saw the snow falling. Piling all of us kids in the car to take us to an amusement park or a picnic. Daddy, what am I going to do without her?"

I went to the funeral with my boyfriend at the time, Bob, whom I had been dating for about a year. Bob was just what I needed at the time. The first time we met, when he sat in and played drums with the band I was singing with, I was immediately attracted to him. He was cute, with brown hair and a mustache. And he was talented—one of the best drummers I'd ever met. Best of all, he made me laugh and feel alive during the year when Mommy was so ill and we knew she was near the end. But when I came home after her funeral, I went into the bedroom I'd shared with my mother for the past three years, shut the door, and called Alfie. We hadn't spoken since we broke up for the last time, more than a year prior. He had asked me to marry him again, and I had refused. The sound of his voice was both warm and pained as I told him we'd buried Mommy today.

"I'll come see you, okay?" he said. "We'll go for a walk on the boardwalk and feed the seagulls like your mom used to do."

*Yes, of course.* That's what I wanted to say. "No, I don't think that's such a good idea," I said, hearing Bob's voice wafting up from the kitchen. I've always regretted that decision more than any other I made in my life, wondering what I'd say to Alfie if I could see him just one last time.

————

I knew it was bad news when Alfie's sister Mary called, not quite a year after Mommy died. "It's Alfie," she said, her voice low and flat. I wanted to hang up, but instead I gripped the phone, a part of me knowing what was coming next.

"My brother was robbed last night," Mary said.

"Robbed?"

"They took his watch, his wallet . . ." Mary was sobbing so hard I could barely hear the rest of what she said. "I'm so sorry, Elissa. He's gone."

I went numb; it couldn't be true. "How can this be happening?" I said. "Tell me this is a bad dream." I thought of Alfie's smile, his sharp sense of humor. I thought of his strong and soothing voice. He could make me laugh like nobody else, even when my mother was at her most ill. He could comfort me like nobody else. I needed him.

I later found out that Alfie had been walking through a seedy part of Philadelphia—why, I still don't know. He was stabbed seventeen times. He was attacked for a watch—one that I gave him—and whatever money he had in his wallet. I couldn't come to grips with the senseless nature of this crime, much less the death of someone who had such a bright future. I couldn't face the fact that I would never see my Alfie again.

I didn't go to Alfie's funeral. A part of me was unable to accept his death; another part of me didn't want to go to another funeral so soon. Two years later, even though I was engaged to Bob, I went to visit his grave in Philadelphia for the first time, running my hand over the name on the headstone, really letting it sink in that he was gone. Even today I still think of him and mourn his loss. Sometimes, I even read those beautiful letters he sent me all those years ago.

I can't really blame Bob for not understanding why I couldn't let it go—why I couldn't let Alfie go. By then, Bob had stopped playing music to focus more on his studies to be an architect, and we were starting to drift apart. He wanted a big house in the suburbs, decorated with designer furniture and expensive artwork. I was happy with my shells from all over the world, scattered under the glass top of our coffee table, and the painting that I had done hanging on the walls.

Bob and I were supposed to be married in less than eight months. I knew it was a mistake, but I couldn't call it off either. My father was thrilled that he was going to walk me down the aisle. Grandma Nellie was so excited, she'd already picked out her dress. My father had put a down payment on the Shadowbrook, a gorgeous Victorian estate in New Jersey surrounded by woods. Our wedding became something happy to focus on after my mother's death; I couldn't rob my family of that. I just couldn't. I remember walking down the aisle, sobbing, everyone thinking it was because I wished Mommy could be there. In truth, I was praying: *Dear God, please forgive me for marrying someone I don't love. Please don't let my mother see this moment.*

The reality is that there's no hiding the fact that you don't love someone. Bob was no fool. He was hurt and resentful, and expressed himself in ways that only moved us further apart. "Why are you spending time writing poetry that nobody's going to read?" he'd ask me disdainfully. And I'll never forget him coming home from work, running a finger over the coffee table and staring at it, then at me. Clearly I was supposed to come home from my job as a lab assistant at the hospital and clean the house by the time he walked through the door. I've never been much of a fighter. Instead, I turned to music to escape from my troubles as I had always done. While Bob was out playing cards with his friends on weekend nights, I went to rock clubs with my friends. And, miraculously, I began waking up from my grief.

One night, bolstered by the encouragement of a big group of friends, I got up the nerve to get up on stage with a local band. I belted out Heart's version of "I've Got the Music in Me," and that was it. There's nothing like the adrenaline rush of being on stage, surrounded by a crowd of people, everyone enjoying riding this wave of happiness that I was actually helping to create. I began performing with friends' bands whenever I could, singing songs by Pat Benatar, Grace Slick, and Chrissie Hynde, strong women I admired. It made me feel powerful to belt out the lyrics written by them—and *happy*. It felt so good to hear the applause of the crowd, to get their positive energy. Even back then, I recognized the healing power of laughter, music, and connecting with other people who shared a passion.

———

My marriage to Bob was officially annulled after two years, in 1982, and I was finally free. I went a little crazy with my freedom. My mother had left the house on 71 Major Avenue to Rita Lu and me when she died, and I bought out my sister's half. I lived there with my stepsister, Danielle, the daughter of my father's second wife and her first husband. Our number one priority was F-U-N. Now, instead of having dinner on the table when and how Bob liked it, I could eat pizza and ice cream at two in the morning and leave my dirty dishes in the sink all night if I wanted to. Not that I actually wanted to, but I could. The main thing I wanted to do now was sing, and I did a lot of that. I also met a lot of guys at the rock clubs where I hung out and performed. At one point I was juggling eleven boyfriends, and I really did care about every one of them. Most of them were musicians; we shared a love of music and life, and they made me laugh again. But I never loved any of them. Those feelings belonged to Alfie.

On the surface I was a free spirit with long dark hair who wore big earrings and tie-dyed colors. But inside I was a ticking time bomb, always feeling like there was something waiting to explode under the surface. It was a strange kind of anxiety, a nervous, uncomfortable restlessness coupled with an overwhelming desire to escape. I could escape for awhile, as long as I was singing—sharing something joyful with the other musicians and the crowd. But when the music stopped, the feelings of pain and sorrow were still there.

In 1986, when I was thirty-three, I made another bad decision: I sold the house on 71 Major Avenue, which had been in our family for more than fifty years, so that I could move to New Smyrna, a quiet town on the central coast of Florida. I was going to buy a concession stand on the beach. I had visions of sitting on the beach and writing songs, walking barefoot in the ocean, just like I had done as a child, walking on South Beach in Staten Island back before the freeway was built.

At first, Florida gave me everything I hoped it would: great weather, tan surfers, and that beautiful ocean. I bought a house close to the beach that I shared with a woman I had worked with in New York and her son, and I spent my days selling hot dogs and renting surf gear while listening to the waves. Unfortunately, I wound up giving away more hot dogs to cute surfer dudes and senior citizens than I sold, and I let elderly ladies sit for free under the umbrellas I was supposed to be renting. And not only did my housemate not pay rent, but her son also totaled my car. Rita Lu kept pleading with me to come back home, and after three years I finally listened. I decided to sell my beach house. That's when I found out it was worth about half of what I'd paid for it. I was humiliated and felt like a complete failure. I was so broke I had to call my sister to borrow money so I could fly back to Staten Island. She never once said, "I told you so," even though she had begged me not to sell our parents' house.

I moved into a tiny room off of the front hall in Rita Lu's house. Grandma Nellie lived in a bedroom down the hall from me. Grandpa Joe had died shortly after Alfie was murdered. We all missed Grandpa terribly but knew he had lived a long and happy life. Grandma still had a lot of life left in her: she was upbeat and loved to laugh, just like her daughter. And she was always going to parties and had lots of friends. "Whatever you do, don't put me in an old folks' home," she used to say to us. "I can't stand being around a bunch of old people."

Living with Grandma and Rita Lu again was almost like being back at 71 Major Avenue, and almost like having my mother with me again. Grandma still cooked and hung wash in the backyard so it would smell nice and fresh. I'd come home from work for lunch, and we'd share some of her homemade chicken soup with pepper and egg sandwiches, just like when I was a kid. She still liked to watch old sitcoms while we ate— reruns of *The Andy Griffith Show* or *Bewitched*. Never the soap operas—they were too depressing.

Another thing I had from my past was my phone number. I'd called the New York telephone company from Florida about a month after I moved there, lonely and already knowing I had made a mistake. I asked if I could keep the old number from 71 Major Avenue on hold for when I moved back. Of course, I couldn't keep it on hold indefinitely, so Rita Lu added a second phone line to her house. That became my phone number and it still is today.

———

Life settled down some when I came home, and I found a stability I hadn't had in a long time. Two radiologists from the hospital where I'd worked before I left were opening a private practice office and asked me to be their assistant. I bought a house with my boyfriend, Tim, a surfer I'd met in Florida and liked well enough. I sang with my friends' bands occasionally on the weekends, or went over to Rita Lu's house for a big Italian dinner courtesy of Grandma Nellie. I wasn't anxious anymore, but I wasn't really happy either. I just was. A voice kept looping in my head: *Why . . . ?* I couldn't stop beating myself up for selling our childhood house, investing in that worthless hot dog stand, marrying a man I didn't love, letting Alfie go. Not being able to keep my father, and then Mommy, from leaving. I still carried around all of these losses, like heavy stones.

The holidays are a difficult time for me because my mother died right before Christmas. Just after Christmas 1992, Grandma Nellie had to go into the hospital. She had developed sciatica, a nerve disorder, and her legs were bothering her. Now, this wasn't so unusual seeing as she was going on ninety-five years old. But Grandma's pain was getting worse, and her two sons thought it would be best to put her in a nursing home until she was feeling better. Rita Lu and I took turns visiting our grandmother almost daily. We polished her nails or tweezed her gray eyebrows in her room. She would never sit on the sofa in the visitors' area. Grandma was very depressed. She asked about our father, whom she loved like her own children, and other relatives. Family was everything to Grandma, and it was literally killing her to be away from us.

After about a month it became clear to everyone, including Grandma Nellie, that her sciatica wasn't getting better. It hurt to put weight on her legs, but in every other respect she was perfectly healthy considering her age. "When are you going to take me home?" she'd ask every time Rita Lu or I visited, getting more restless every day. "I'm too young to be in here with all of these old people!" We weren't the decision makers, but I promised that I'd get my grandma back home again—and I meant it. She'd taken care of Rita Lu and me for all of these years, and now it was our turn. It was the right thing to do.

My sister and I started researching private nurses and trying to convince our uncles we could take care of Grandma Nellie at home, where she belonged. And every day we'd visit our grandmother and reassure her, but she was clearly getting more and more depressed. Six weeks after she entered the nursing home, Grandma Nellie died of congestive heart failure. It was Valentine's Day, and there had been a terrible ice storm for five days that kept Rita Lu and me from visiting. I'll always believe that she died of a broken heart, lonely and sad. She missed her family. And I'll always feel guilty that I couldn't keep my promise to bring her home. I knew my sister and my uncles were hurting just as bad as I was. I didn't want to add to their burden, so, instead, I kept quiet. It kept my pain in the same place deep inside where I was still grieving for Mommy and Alfie, praying that one day it would just disappear.

———

It was a hot June day, four months after Grandma died, and the bank lobby was stuffy and crowded, the line moving in slow motion. I was waiting to make a deposit for the radiologists I worked for, just like every Friday afternoon. People were grumbling, complaining about the heat and service—which never helps anything, right? I remember my shirt was starting to stick to my back, and I kept looking out the windows wishing I was at the beach. Then, out of nowhere, I didn't just wish I was somewhere else but I *had* to be somewhere else. I had to get out of there. My life depended on it. But how could I leave before making the deposit? What would I tell the doctors? And what would all of these people think if I just bolted out the door? Now I was really sweating. My heart was pumping faster and faster. I felt it in my head and my ears, throughout my entire body. I was trying to take my pulse in my wrist, and it was so fast I couldn't even count it. I was terrified. My legs seemed to be turning into Jell-O, and then my entire body was weak. I bent over and put my hands on my knees, pretending to nonchalantly scratch myself, just to stay on my feet. I imagined that everyone was staring at me—whether it was true or not—and they all knew I was on the verge of fainting.

I think the fear of embarrassment—passing out in front of all of those people—actually saved me that day. I walked up to the teller station, leaned on the counter with my sweaty palms, and pasted a smile on my face. Just like I'd done for my mother all those years she was ill. Just like I'd done after Alfie died. Looking back, I can see that I'd been wearing a big smile as a mask for more than twenty-five years.

I was hoping this crazy reaction—which I didn't recognize then as a panic attack—was just a one-time thing. But what if it wasn't? And of course, my constant worrying just made the anxiety even worse. I couldn't sleep and my heart was constantly racing. The panic attacks kept coming, and the worst part was that I never knew when the monster would strike: at work, at the mall, when I went to the grocery store. My friends began wondering why I didn't want to go out for a bite to eat after work or to the movies on a Friday night, or even to the music clubs. Even though I was skilled at hiding my emotions after so many years of practice, now I was always afraid. When would the next attack happen? What if people found out? Why was this happening? I was tired all of the time and worried that something might be physically wrong with me. At the same time I couldn't admit to anyone—not even my sister—that my life had become a living hell.

The only place I felt safe was in my townhouse, where I now lived alone. I spent a lot of time in my bedroom, sitting on my bed beside my Newfoundland, Obie, who had an incredible calming effect, just inhaling his love. Soothing flute and strings music in the background reminded me of the ebb and flow of the ocean. I would light a single candle on my bedside table, which would cast shadows on the wall. I wrote about feeling lonely and scared—poems, songs, and journal entries—and I prayed a lot too, sometimes in letters to God. But I never lost faith during this dark period. I never asked, *Why are you doing this to me, God?* I just kept asking for His help in understanding what was happening and how to free myself, how to get back to the outgoing person who loved life and people instead of avoiding both, hiding in my room.

Not only was I stressed out and depressed, but I was also feeling physically ill—I was exhausted and my heart palpitations kept getting worse. Finally, after this went on for about six months, I went to see a cardiologist in the complex of doctors where I worked. The tests all came back normal, but the doctor said he was concerned about how fast my heart was beating. I was actually having a panic attack in his office. He asked if anything was bothering me, and I mentioned that my grandmother had died. He recommended a psychologist, Steve, whom I wound up seeing for two years. Steve helped me to understand what I was going through. As he explained it: "All of your losses were piling up in a basket, adding weight, because you never really processed and let go of any of your grief. You are grieving your mother's long painful illness, Alfie's murder, and losing the childhood home you were so attached to. And then when your grandmother died, that was the tipping point. That's when the weight became too much and that basket broke—something in your soul broke."

Steve put a name to what I'd been feeling on and off for fifteen years: depression. He said the panic attacks, the loss of interest in my friends and my singing, and the fear of being around other people were all part of the same package. But I didn't want to admit he was right; I was stronger than that. I spent another four years denying my feelings, fighting the label of depression, and digging myself deeper and deeper into a very dark hole. It took a miracle to help me climb out. That miracle came in the form of a fifteen-year-old boy who, at the same time that I was lost in depression, was fighting battles that made mine pale in comparison.

## CHAPTER FOUR

# The Wrecking Ball Hits Bosnia

*Maglaj, Bosnia, December 1993*

Eleven-year-old Kenan Malkic woke up early, just after dawn, to go get water from the pump at the side of his apartment building. He wanted his pregnant mother to be able to wash up when she awoke. Hot baths were a luxury; the electricity worked for just a few hours at a time, and you could never predict when that would be or for how long. The Serbs had surrounded Maglaj two months earlier, cutting off all land supplies and bombing the remaining government buildings, utilities, the train station—and everything in between. But Kenan couldn't think about that now. According to his father, the fighting was settling down for at least a few days while the Serbs regrouped after their last attack. Miralem had gotten a message to his family yesterday morning through a soldier who was home on leave from the army base where Miralem was also stationed: it was finally safe for Kenan and Aida to come up from the basement.

Living in the cold, damp concrete-floored basement—three small rooms and two slightly larger rooms—off and on had become a way of life for Kenan and Aida and the twenty other families in their apartment complex during the past nineteen months. All of the families spent days or weeks there when the fighting heated up. The children slept on mattresses on the cement floor, the adults mostly on the plastic lounge chairs they usually took to the beach. If it was quiet, you could run upstairs to your apartment to go to the bathroom or grab a fresh change of clothes, but only for a few minutes at a time.

Kenan and his friends played by candlelight down there, cards or imaginary games of the times when life had been blissfully ordinary: "school" and "house." Meanwhile, the adults sat in the big room, talking, listening to the radio, or watching TV during the short periods when there was electricity. The radio was everything in that basement—the only link to the outside world. Miralem had hooked up a car battery in the Malkic dining room that they usually charged by plugging into the wall, but when the electricity wasn't working they had to get creative. So, Kenan's father hooked up the big battery to the back of a stationary bike a neighbor had, and Kenan pedaled for hours to keep that battery charged and the radio going. When there was silence, it was unbearable: the only sound was grenades exploding outside.

Everyone tried to keep things light in whatever ways they could. The children made up shows for the adults, with Kenan acting as the master of ceremonies and DJ. The other children choreographed dances, some using martial arts moves they'd seen in the movie *Teenage Mutant Ninja Turtles*, which had come to Sarajevo just before the war began.

Now, as the first rays of sunlight poked through Kenan's window, he pulled on the T-shirt and jeans hanging on a chair by his bed and opened his dresser drawer to take inventory. If the sun stayed out today, maybe he'd take some laundry out to the concrete slab and pump at the side of the building to wash his clothes. Maybe the squash in the garden would be big enough that he could pick one for dinner. He was so sick of the heavy flat bread his mother made on the woodstove in the basement using potatoes, rice, and beans. What he wouldn't give for a pita filled with meat and cheese, or baklava! Well, at least the United Nations had finally made an airdrop of food after almost a month of waiting, not that those nondescript meals in foil bags were so great. That night, Grandma Hiba was coming over to cook dinner for the family. She had a way of combining ingredients that you wouldn't think tasted good together—beans and lentils, dehydrated UN carrots and peas, some spices—and making it taste delicious. Most important, his father was coming home; that's all that really mattered.

Miralem was now gone for weeks at a time, stationed in Tesanj, the next town over on the front line of the war. No personal transportation was allowed, keeping the roads clear for the military, so he had to walk home five or six hours through the mountains unless he could hitch a ride with an ambulance or army vehicle. Kenan was used to being the man of the family while his father was away, and he took his responsibility very seriously—especially since his mother was expecting a baby. Carrying the bucket of water into the bathroom, he ran his hand over the wall for the light switch. He smiled as the room lit up, pleased with his handiwork. A few days earlier he had found a phone wire and hooked it up to the battery in the living room, running it under the carpet and to the bathroom, attaching it to a switch on the wall and a single lightbulb so that Aida could turn on a light even when the electricity was out.

Aida was in the kitchen, mixing just enough powdered milk to pour a glass for Kenan and one for herself. "Good morning," Kenan said, kissing his mother's cheek, looking longingly at the UN rations of flour, sugar, and one lone chocolate bar on the counter.

"*Dobro jutro,*" Aida said, checking the stove with one hand, the other hand pushing the chocolate farther away from her son, out of the reach of temptation. "I'm going to mix up a cake, on faith. We need a real celebration when your father comes home tonight."

All of Kenan's relatives in the area were coming over for the first time since the heavy fighting began. Both of his uncles and their wives, his cousins, and both sets of grandparents were going to be arriving soon. Aida was in such a good mood, humming as she took out the mixing bowl and measuring cups, that Kenan cleared his throat. "So Dad really thinks the fighting should stop for a few days, maybe longer?"

"Mmm." Aida was busy measuring flour, her brow wrinkled in concentration.

"So, I was thinking . . . ," Kenan began, crossing his fingers behind his back for luck. "Maybe I can go to radio school today?"

Aida looked up from the mixing bowl at her son's pleading eyes. She wanted to say yes, knowing how much Kenan loved going to the radio station where his sixth grade teacher had been broadcasting lessons for the students since it became too dangerous to attend school. For awhile, children were meeting in the basement of an apartment house in each district. That was before the Serbs somehow caught wind of this and shelled a school meeting at an apartment building last March. Three children were killed, and more than a dozen were injured. What if they found out that Kenan and some of his friends were helping their teacher at the radio station? It seemed unlikely, but then again Aida had learned to expect the worst these days.

"I'm sorry, *ljubavi*." Aida shook her head and kissed Kenan's cheek. Her son was fighting back tears, and she knew this wasn't just about going to the radio station. He missed his friends; he missed his life. She reached for the chocolate bar, meaning to offer a square as an olive branch. But Kenan quickly put his plate and glass in the sink and left the room.

At lunch, over peanut butter sandwiches, Aida tried again. "Maybe tomorrow you can go to the radio station, when your father's here to walk with you."

Kenan grinned, throwing his arms around his mother's round middle. "Thanks, Mom. You're the best." He hummed as he went out on the balcony to check the now clean laundry that was slowly drying over the railing.

A few minutes later, Kenan heard the phone ring, and his mother joined him on the balcony. "Your father," Aida mouthed to him, then said into the phone, "We'll hold supper for you. The electricity just came on and Mama's on her way over, so say a prayer we won't have half-baked food. Yes, I love you too."

Just a few minutes after Aida hung up the phone, a loud ping cracked the air: metal hitting metal, and then glass shattering inside the kitchen. Aida put one hand on her stomach, drawing

Kenan toward her with the other hand. "Dear God," she whispered, her voice shaky.

They both stood there, paralyzed with fear for what seemed like a long time before going inside to investigate: A glass was shattered on the kitchen counter. The wall above the sink was cracked, a bullet lodged firmly in the plaster. "It must have ricocheted off the railing," Kenan said, examining the small round hole, which was still smoking. Suddenly, he hugged his mother tightly and began to cry, burrowing his face in her warm neck. She had been drinking from this glass, standing right in this same spot, when she answered the phone.

"Kenan," Aida said, lifting his face in her hands to look at him straight on. Her fair skin was chalky white, and Kenan knew his mother was scared. "Thank God everyone's okay." That was it, she didn't say anything else. Not when his grandmother came over a few minutes later. Not when more relatives arrived throughout the afternoon. Not when Miralem returned in the early evening and kissed his wife, telling her how good it was to be home again. Kenan showed his father the hole in the kitchen wall and told him what happened, leaving out the part about his pregnant mother nearly being killed. As soon as his father returned home it was as if everything had just been a bad dream.

*September 1994*

It was a crisp fall day, two years after the war began and just shy of Kenan's twelfth birthday. There hadn't been a grenade attack on Maglaj in several days. By this time, people had learned to do what they needed to do—shopping or just going outside for a few hours of fresh air—when they could. There were areas in town that were safe, like the field behind the apartment building where the Malkics lived, which was in a valley and protected. After radio school, Kenan and his friends sometimes gathered for a game of soccer. That day, he was lacing up his cleats in his room, glancing at the newspaper clipping on his bulletin board. There was a photo of the Bosnian National Soccer Team—sweaty, filthy, and grinning wildly. Kenan's father had taken him to that game a few months earlier, the first professional soccer game played in Sarajevo in two years.

Kenan and Miralem had been among the thousands of people cheering as the Bosnian team scored again and again, defeating the UN four to zero. People were hopeful for the first time in months, even though they were standing in the shattered shell of what was once an Olympic stadium. The grass field was mostly dirt, but level. All around it were jagged holes from grenades and land mines. The clubhouse where concessions were once sold was a collection of charred bricks and broken windows. And yet, the Bosnian people stood and cheered for their team. What else did they have?

As Kenan stood on the field behind his home, he shifted his weight from foot to foot as he waited to pounce on the ball when it came his way. He pulled at the collar of his blue and gold jersey—the colors of the Bosnian National Soccer Team—wishing he had worn a T-shirt. It was unseasonably warm and he was sweating. "Look alive, Malkic," someone shouted from downfield, and Kenan lunged to catch the black-and-white ball soaring toward him. He was tall and wiry, with long legs and quick reactions—the perfect goalie. There was no net, so if the ball got past Kenan—like now—it rolled into the tall grass behind the field. He went to retrieve it as usual, bending down to pick it up. He was shocked by an incredible force.

He felt the force first in his mouth, and then he went flying through the air. *Oh, crap, my teeth are knocked out*, he thought, lying facedown in the dirt, not even noticing the pain in the rest of his body. He ran his tongue around to check his teeth and there was this weird taste—blood, dirt, and gunpowder. As hard as he tried to spit it out, the taste just kept coming.

Then there was shouting, screaming. Next Kenan was being lifted onto a stretcher by two men and put into a vehicle. "We're taking you to the hospital, son," one of the men told him. "Just hang on."

Kenan recognized the voice as belonging to Addo, his mother's younger brother, although he couldn't open his eyes to look at him. "It's me, your uncle Addo, Kenan," he said. He later found out that Addo was so shaken up that someone else had to drive the ambulance to the hospital while he sat next to his nephew, holding his arm.

Kenan came to in the emergency room, his eyes glued shut from the blast, the sounds of people shouting and scrambling around him, ripping off his soccer jersey and jeans.

"Find some anesthesia. Whatever you can find!"

"Cut up some sheets if you can't find gauze—we need something to stop the bleeding."

"If that generator blows . . ."

"Don't let me die, just don't let me die," Kenan prayed, not even realizing he was speaking aloud.

A soft, sweet voice at the side of his head whispered, "Don't worry, just sleep."

It was like the voice of an angel, so calm and reassuring. Kenan just let himself sink into unconsciousness. Nobody was sure if he'd ever wake up again.

Meanwhile, Aida sat in the hospital waiting room, one hour, then two, four. She tried calling Miralem, but he wasn't answering his phone, probably out on maneuvers. Her hands kept methodically rubbing her stomach, as if still protecting her baby. She'd been on bed rest during the last three months of her pregnancy after some spotting and cramping, sleeping in the middle of the living room because she couldn't even walk downstairs to the basement. Kenan had insisted on sleeping with her, curled up by her side. "I don't think this baby likes me," he'd joke when the baby was restless. "He keeps kicking me." Neighbors would sometimes bring Aida a coveted apple or pear; fruit and vegetables were scarce, meat unheard of, during the eight months that Maglaj was surrounded by the Serbs. She began avoiding looking in mirrors, scared by the pale, gaunt face she saw looking back.

One night, at just over eight months along, Aida awoke terrified, her arms numb. "Kenan, *ljubavi*," she said calmly, even though her heart was racing, "Call Grandma Hiba to come stay with you. I need to go to the hospital."

"No, I'm coming with you," Kenan had insisted. The last time the ambulance had come and taken his mother to Tesanj he'd been so worried he could barely eat or sleep for the three days she'd been gone. He rode in the back of the ambulance with his mother, across the bumpy mountain roads to avoid the Serbs. The ride should have taken thirty minutes—it took closer to two hours. But by the time they arrived at the hospital, Miralem was waiting.

Now, being in the same emergency room where she'd been ten months earlier was unsettling for Aida. The same ER where the doctor had told her that they needed to operate and take baby Adnen out immediately because both of their lives were in danger. "Take Kenan home, I'll be fine," Aida recalled telling her husband, even though her body felt on fire with fever. She didn't want Kenan or Miralem to worry; they'd both been through enough. She went to sleep that night assured by a nurse that she had delivered a healthy baby boy. The next day, when Miralem returned, the doctor told them both that the baby had been too weak to survive. The hospital generator failed, and there was no heat for the incubator that could have saved her newborn son's life.

"Please, God, don't take my Kenan too," Aida prayed aloud. She jumped, feeling a hand on her shoulder. A doctor wearing green scrubs and a surgical mask stood over her. His eyes appeared empty, as if drained of emotion.

"I'm sorry, Mrs. Malkic. We did what we could . . ." His voice trailed off as he sighed heavily and took off his mask.

"He's alive," Aida said firmly. Her son had to be alive.

"Yes, but just barely," the doctor said.

"He'll make it. My son is strong."

"Mrs. Malkic, you must prepare yourself for the worst. Kenan's lost a lot of blood, and we had to amputate both of his arms just below the elbows and his left leg." Aida remembered being in the operating room, just barely sedated because anesthesia was scarce. "He's okay, Kenan's okay," she whispered, holding her stomach.

The doctor shook his head. "The chances aren't good that the boy will survive such massive trauma. Perhaps that's for the best."

Aida was weak with exhaustion, yet suddenly the petite, gentle woman grabbed the doctor's shirt and pushed him against the wall. "Don't you ever say that again!" she yelled into his face. "My son will live."

The short, stocky man was visibly shaken and Aida stepped back, putting her hand to her mouth, shaking her head, tears streaming down her face.

"As I said, you must prepare yourself," the doctor repeated wearily. "If Kenan does survive, he will never have a happy, normal life."

Aida slumped into a chair, dropped her head into her hands, and cried. The doctor was right. What kind of life would an eleven-year-old boy missing both arms and a leg have? Even before the war there were few prosthetics available in Eastern Europe, no physical therapy facilities. They'd be lucky to find a wheelchair for their son. Then, her phone rang. She knew it must be Miralem returning her calls. She pulled herself together and answered, calmly explaining to her husband that Kenan had been in an accident. "It was terrible, but he's alive," she said. "Thank God our son is alive, and he's going to be okay. We'll make sure of it."

———

"Put me back to sleep, I don't want to wake up." Those were the first words that Kenan spoke to his mother when he opened his eyes ten days after his surgery and saw that he had no arms and was missing a leg. He'd been heavily sedated, his eyes crusted shut by the gunpowder blast, his entire body scarred and encased in pain. The doctors had thought it was best to let him sleep; his young body had been through so much. Every so often he'd wake up and ask his mother, "Why do my arms feel short? What happened to my hands?"

"They're fine, just bandaged," Aida said. Her son would find out the truth soon enough. She sat by his bedside, all day and all night for ten days, dozing only briefly, as other people—children and adults—came and shared this room with seven beds. As patients died in the beds surrounding her son, she thanked God that her son was alive and prayed that he would be spared his eyesight so that he could have some chance for normalcy.

Now, Kenan stared at the bandages tightly wrapped around what was left of his arms: two stumps propped up on pillows. He could feel his left leg throbbing and tried to wiggle his toes even though he somehow knew they weren't there. "There is no future," he said flatly, as if he'd heard the doctors telling his mother the same thing. "Put me back to sleep again."

Kenan cried for two straight days after waking up. Aida sat and held him; there was nothing she or Miralem could say to console their son.

"This is terrible, but crying isn't going to change it," his father told him gently. "All we can do now is figure out how you can live your life, day to day. The alternative is much worse."

After two days, Kenan stopped crying. He wanted to make

his father proud and wipe the worried look from his mother's face. "Don't worry, I'll be okay," he said, and that actually seemed possible when his parents told him that he could get prosthetic limbs and learn to do all of the things he'd done before.

But there were hours, and even days, during the next few weeks when Kenan lay curled up on his side and wouldn't talk to anyone or even look at them. He was moved to a private room after three weeks, which seemed to help a little. And then one day a boy about Kenan's age came into his room in a wheelchair. He was also a land mine victim and had lost both of his legs.

"You're so lucky," the boy said.

"Lucky?" Kenan raised his bandaged arms, as if to show the boy that he was mistaken.

"You have a family to take care of you."

"And you?"

"I have parents and three sisters," the boy said softly. "After the accident my mom came to the hospital and said to me, 'I can't take care of you. I'm sorry, but you can't come home again.'"

Kenan's visitor made an impression.

Aida's cousin Safija, who lived in Toronto, called every night during the last month of Kenan's stay in the hospital, and Aida helped her son to get out of bed and wait by the phone in the hallway for these updates. Safija and her husband, Allen, who worked as a cardiologist, raised money for cosmetic surgery for Kenan's scarred face as well as his leg. There was even a school in Canada for children who had lost limbs that was willing to give Kenan a scholarship. Aida knew it was virtually impossible to leave the country while the war was still raging, but she never spoke of this to Kenan. What he needed now, even before the surgery and the new limbs, was hope. Sometimes, that's the best medicine in the world.

## CHAPTER FIVE

# Getting Back to Normal

*December 1995*

Two years after Grandma Nellie died, when I was in the midst of my battle with depression and anxiety, fighting for just a moment of normalcy, Kenan was doing the same thing. Both of our worlds had been destroyed—the difference was that his had literally exploded and there was no way to hide his hurt.

Kenan was released from the hospital after two months and sent home to relearn how to get dressed, bathe, and feed himself—and all of the other mundane things we take for granted—using the bandaged stumps that ended just below his elbows that he calls his hands. He was lucky to have his elbows, physical therapists would later say, because the moveable joint works like a wrist, allowing him to manipulate the inches of forearms below. Even before the war there were no resources for prosthetics in Bosnia, let alone physical therapy, anywhere near where the Malkics lived. Aida and Miralem tried to help their son as best they could, knowing it would never be enough.

When Kenan came home, each day was a series of challenges from the time that he got out of bed. It wasn't long before he tired of his mother helping him do everything. "I'm not a baby. I want to feed myself," he told her one morning at breakfast.

"I know, but you can't," Aida said.

"Sure I can. Just tape my fork to my elbow and I'll scoop the eggs from the plate into my mouth." It took some practice, but after Kenan got the hang of using a fork he used the same technique for using a spoon to eat soup at lunch and for brushing his teeth at night. A few days later, Kenan asked his mother to lay an oversize T-shirt out on his bed. He knelt on the floor, taking the bottom of the shirt in his teeth and maneuvering his head into it, then wriggling it over his shoulders. Within a few weeks, he was getting dressed and feeding himself, showering using a chair, and using a wheelchair by pushing off with just one leg. "I'm a big boy. I can do it myself," he said over and over, taking to heart the advice his father had given him in the hospital, to make the most of what he had instead of dwelling on all he had lost. Kenan amazed everyone around him with all he could do, his strength, and his positive attitude.

"You don't have to go to school," Aida had told her son when he came home from the hospital, wanting to protect him from the stares and questions. "You can stay home as long as you want."

"Mom, are you crazy?" Kenan responded. "I want to go to school, to college, to do important things. Do you know what happens if you don't go to school?"

"You're right," Aida said softly. Of course her son was right. There were many other people in town who had lost limbs to hidden land mines, some in their own front yards. Most had lost all hope, falling into drugs and alcohol, giving up on their families and any kind of future. *Your son will never have a happy, normal life.* The words of that doctor kept echoing in Aida's head. She couldn't let that happen. At the same time, Kenan couldn't go to school and be independent, the way he wanted to, without prosthetics. He would need someone to take him and his heavy wheelchair to school in a car, someone to carry him and the chair up the stairs, help him into his desk and out again. This would break her son's spirit. She knew it would.

It took Miralem and Safija's husband, Allen, a month to arrange the travel details with the Turkish Red Cross and Canadian Armed Forces: a helicopter from Zenica, a city near Maglaj, to a coastal town in Bosnia, then a Canadian Military plane across the Adriatic Sea to Italy, and another small plane to Toronto. This was the first time Aida and her son had traveled outside of Europe, and they would spend eighteen months in a country where they knew little of the language, with only Safija and Allen's family to rely on. Aida was lonely in Canada, and when she returned home, she barely recognized her husband at the airport. But she would do it all again to save her son's life.

*Toronto, June 1995*

Kenan tossed back and forth on the bed in the guest room of his aunt and uncle's house, which he'd been sharing with his mother for six months. It was no use, he couldn't sleep. He sat up and flipped on the lamp to admire the sturdy plastic leg leaning against the end of the bed that had been delivered that afternoon. The grown-ups were watching TV, so they would never know if he disobeyed the doctor's orders and just tried it on. He sat up and appraised the stitches on his knee from the

recent surgery to straighten out a bone: the skin was still pur-
plish, and he could feel it throbbing. But what would it hurt to
just try the leg on? He'd dreamed of this leg for nearly a year,
and what he could do with it: ride his bike with his friends, go
to school, maybe even play goalie again. This leg was going to
change his life—it had to.

He kicked at the two prosthetic arms—plastic limbs with
hooks for hands—on the rug that had been such a disappointment. He had gone through six months of painful therapy,
daily sessions at the hospital where they soaked and massaged
the stumps below his elbows where he'd lost limbs, breaking
down the thick scars in order to properly fit the prosthetics.
Kenan had endured the pain by gritting his teeth and squeezing his eyes shut, picturing real hands with moving fingers,
but, of course, his new limbs weren't like that. The first time he
put on his new hands it was horrible. They were heavy and
awkward and itched so badly that he had to pour water into
them so that his skin was less irritated. He was still getting
used to them, and he hated that the physical therapists insisted
he use the hooks to do things that were actually easier to do
with what remained of his real arms. Just yesterday, he'd gotten in big trouble when the head of the school called his mom
in for a conference about what she called his "stubbornness
streak."

"Just do what they ask of you," Aida had begged her son.
"Don't make trouble."

"Look, I'm not a stubborn person. I just know better," Kenan
said to his mother, just as he had said to the physical therapist.
The therapist was insisting that he use special silverware with

plastic handles that fit over the hooks, even though Kenan could grab regular spoons and forks between his severed forearms and use his own limbs to eat like everyone else. The only one of the dozens of gizmos they taught him how to use over the eighteen months Kenan spent in Canada that he kept was an extra-long shoehorn, which he gave to his grandfather. What bothered him most was that many of these gadgets had to be put on his hooks by someone else. More than anything, Kenan wanted to be independent.

"Honey, you're still a child," Aida said. "You don't always know best."

"All I told them was the truth, Mom. If you haven't lost three limbs, don't tell me that you know better how to do things. You and Dad are the ones who taught me to help myself, right?"

*She couldn't argue with that*, Kenan thought, as he scooted toward the end of the bed to get a closer look at the leg. He moved his upper arm over the smooth plastic calf, ankle, and foot. How would it actually feel against his skin? Would it be heavy and uncomfortable like the arms? A shiver of doubt ran through Kenan, his breath coming faster as more and more questions tumbled through his mind. What if they were right? What if he would never really be able to do everything he wanted to do on his own? He could manage without the arms. But the leg? He had to have the leg. If he couldn't walk, he'd never be able to go back to school or play with his friends. He'd never find his way back to normal. What if he never had a normal life again?

He couldn't let these questions and doubts grab hold of him, twisting themselves around his throat like tight choking hands.

That's what had happened one of the first nights he'd spent in Toronto, lying on his cot in the dark, worrying about the future. His heart had started beating wildly and his breath caught in his throat, scaring him so badly that he jumped out of bed and crawled downstairs to where his mother, Safija, and Allen were talking in the living room. "You're just not used to your surroundings," Allen had said, patting Kenan on the back and telling him to go back to sleep. "You'll be okay in the morning."

But the next day Kenan was still anxious and afraid of what his future might hold. He thought of his father, whom he missed terribly, telling him that nothing was going to change what had happened. Even the best prosthetics weren't going to make him whole again, and he had no choice but to learn to deal with it. Kenan didn't realize that he'd had a panic attack—he couldn't put a name to what had happened—but he was certain that he didn't want to ever feel that way again. Now, hoisting the prosthetic leg onto his knee and strapping it into place, he reminded himself that he did have a choice. At the moment that meant figuring out how to walk on this new leg.

Kenan stood gingerly, testing his weight on the new leg, wincing as the plastic rubbed against his tender skin. *Not too bad*, he told himself. At least it wasn't nearly as painful as when they had broken down the scar tissue on his knee. And it wasn't nearly as painful as the looks of pity he'd turned away from so many times during the past year. He hobbled over to the full-length mirror on the closet door, both grinning and grimacing as he tried a few goalie moves. He tried putting all his weight on the new limb, jumping just a little as if reaching up toward a basketball hoop, and toppled back against the bed.

"Is everything okay in here?" Aida asked, cracking open the door moments later after hearing the commotion from downstairs.

"Fine. Everything is going to be fine," Kenan replied, back in his bed, rubbing his sore knee under the blanket. Next to him was his new leg, which he kept close by his side all night.

Kenan loved being in Toronto for the next year and a half, where it was easy for him to blend into the throngs of people too busy to give him more than a glance. But when he came home to the small town of Maglaj in the summer of 1996, at age thirteen, people stopped and kept their eyes glued to him and Aida as they walked by. They usually didn't say anything, but it was worse for Kenan when they did. "What a tragedy," they would say, shaking their heads. Or, "I feel so bad for you; it must be terrible."

Kenan learned to smile tightly and walk on, the anger churned up by these words of pity only making him more determined and stronger. His dad helped him learn to ride his bike again. His mother taught him to hold a pencil with his prosthetic hand so that he could enter the eighth grade with his friends. Kenan's teacher had high expectations for him: on the first day of school, she scolded him in front of the entire class because his handwriting was so bad. He credits her as the reason his penmanship became perfect.

I've always been amazed that Kenan so clearly saw his options. On the day I was standing in line at the bank, feeling those crazed moths fluttering in my chest and praying I wouldn't pass out—and during the four years that followed—it never occurred to me that I had any kind of choice. The panic attacks were in charge, and it seemed like I was powerless to fight them. Kenan was the person who taught me that I had endless strength and a boundless capacity to accomplish whatever I wanted to do. But it didn't happen overnight.

———

By early 1997, I had to admit it: I was in a deep, dark hole and I needed to find a way out. For four years I'd been hiding my fear, never knowing when a full-blown panic attack would come on. *If I can just get dressed and make it into my car. If I can just drive to work. If I can just look happy and normal while I say my round of good mornings at the office and then I can keep busy in the filing room until I settle down.* I was okay as long as I could take a stack of X-rays and other paperwork into the back room, but my legs would start to buckle under me while using the Xerox machine out in the open where everyone could see me. Could they sense that I had a secret? Did they know, just by looking at me?

This is how many days went, and I returned home at night totally spent. My house was the only place I felt safe, and yet it had also become like a prison. My body also felt like a prison. Who was this person who didn't enjoy spending time with friends or going out to listen to music, let alone singing? One of my few pleasures was watching old reruns of the television shows of my youth—*The Donna Reed Show, The Honeymooners, The Andy Griffith Show.* I'd think of how Grandma, Mommy, Rita Lu, and I had all piled onto the couch in our living room, laughing aloud at these jokes that now seemed so corny. So simple. I longed for those simpler, happier days. Somehow, I needed to regain control of my life and find my joy again. I needed to find a way to reconnect with people and my passion.

My chance came in June, when my friend Danny asked me to write a song for a charity event he was putting together. I loved what he was doing: WABC radio station was doing a diner tour, broadcasting from a location in each of the five boroughs, including Staten Island's popular Colonnade Diner. Danny had asked a DJ if he'd announce that people could stop by when they were broadcasting live to donate toys and school supplies. Danny would then send all of the donations to children in war-torn Bosnia through the Bosnia and Herzegovina Mission to the United Nations. Danny wanted to help find someone to produce the song so we could sell the recording and raise money as well. As much as I wanted to get involved, I didn't sign on right away—I couldn't. First of all, I didn't know much about Bosnia except what I'd read in the news: that a war had just ended there. Second, Danny wanted me to perform the song I wrote at the diner; that was the real stopper. "This is a great opportunity for you to really shine," Danny said, trying to coax me into agreeing, confused about my hesitation. I pictured myself up on stage, singing a song I'd written, and felt a space open up in my heart where the old me was hiding. But then I saw myself breaking into a sweat, my legs buckling, not even being able to run off the stage. I told Danny no thanks, even though my heart was screaming *Yes!*

I went to the library and looked up newspaper articles in *The New York Times* from the past few years about what had been happening in Bosnia. Millions of people—mostly Muslims and some Croatians—had been forced from their homes by the Serbs, and more than one hundred thousand people had been murdered. Beautiful centuries-old buildings in Sarajevo were now bombed-out shells; homes in the once-peaceful farming towns in the mountains were demolished. But it was the photos of the children that really got to me: so innocent and helpless. I wanted to help. Even in my darkest hour, I never lost confidence in my ability to write poetry and song lyrics, and I thought this was my chance—in a small way—to actually help bring awareness to these kids who didn't even have coloring books or pencils.

I called Danny and told him I'd write the song lyrics, but I couldn't sing at the event. "Just think about it," he said. "You don't want to perform the song live?" And I did think about it during the next few weeks while I was writing "Let's Do a Miracle" with composer Pat D'Ambrosio. I thought about how much I wanted to sing, and also how much I wanted to be part of something bigger than the fear that had been controlling my life for so long. I thought about the "clubhouse" in our garage at 71 Major Avenue, and how much fun we'd had putting together those shows. I thought about how proud Mommy would have been of me. She was the one always telling me I had a gift for writing songs and making people happy. *You're my ray of sunshine*, I heard her saying—I wanted to feel like that again. But still, there was no way that I could perform in front of people, and that knowledge tore me apart.

I felt both my mother and grandmother with me the day that Pat and I went to the Colonnade Diner to be interviewed by a DJ from WABC and hear our song "Let's Do a Miracle" played for the first time on air. I was so proud of what I'd helped to create, both the song and a bridge between my community on Staten Island and families halfway across the globe. At the same time, it took all of my strength to quash down the anxiety fluttering in the pit of my stomach, preparing to take flight into my chest. As dozens of parents and their kids flowed in and out of the diner, dropping off toys, I listened to the words of our song, singing along in my head while the DJ played the recording.

*Little faces with giant tears, shivering with fright,*
*it's been going on for years.*
*Weak and weary with nothing to eat,*
*they sleep in despair on a bed of concrete.*

*Hoping that someone like us will step in,*
*raise their spirits high and put an end to this sin.*

*Let's help the children, let's lend a hand,*
*they could be ours, they're our fellow man.*
*God bless the children, together we can*
*do a miracle for the Bosnian land.*

*And if only we can dry their tears, wipe off their frowns,*
*ease all their fears.*
*If for a moment we could feel their pain,*
*then we'd understand we have so much to gain.*

*Look in your heart for a place if you dare.*
*Put yourself aside and show the children you care.*

*Let's help the children, let's lend a hand.*
*They could be ours . . . They're our fellow man.*
*God bless the children, together we can*
*do a miracle for the Bosnian land.*

I kept focused on the feeling that I was sharing a little piece of my old neighborhood, the big extended Italian family that gathered at 71 Major Avenue with the rest of the world. I could see Mommy and Grandma Nellie smiling in agreement. And to my relief and surprise, those fluttering moths in my stomach actually settled down.

In that moment, sitting at the diner, listening to "Let's Do a Miracle," I realized that this was what I'd been waiting for all along: the music to begin again. For the first time in years, I started to hear a faint melody and I wanted it to keep swelling, growing stronger. Little did I know how loud and powerful— how joyful—that song was going to become.

The diner broadcast was modestly successful—lots of people dropped off school supplies and toys, and some children donated a few dollars—but during the weeks after the event I kept thinking that there was something more I could do. I called a few of my old contacts in the music business and got some mild interest in publishing the song, but it wasn't something that was going to happen overnight. So, instead, I called the office of Muhamed Sacirbey, Bosnia's ambassador to the UN. He had supported the fund-raising effort, although he was out of the country on the day of the actual event. We'd never met, but I'd seen his name and photo in the newspaper plenty. To my amazement, he agreed to meet with me.

Making that phone call to Mo's secretary from the safety of my kitchen table was one thing, but going to the UN building in New York City was a completely different story. I went into the city with Danny and Pat; I never could have done it on my own. My heart was racing as I took the elevator up to Mo's office—but as soon as I met Mo, he put me completely at ease. He smiled warmly and seemed genuinely glad to see me—like we were already old friends.

Sitting across from this handsome and confident man who regularly met with world leaders and diplomats, I didn't have a clue that in some ways he was no different than me. Months later, he would tell me that he was also grieving and trying to figure out how to heal. He was glad that the war had ended, but worried about the future. He worried that his efforts wouldn't help enough people.

Mo had received a letter from Kenan's father when he was feeling particularly vulnerable. Miralem had sent this letter to the Red Cross and a number of other agencies with no luck—he was desperate to get new prosthetics for his son because he'd outgrown the ones he had received in Canada. Usually, Mo passed those kinds of letters along to other members of the team who could try to help. But this time, instead, he had put the letter and photo of Kenan lying in his hospital bed right after his accident in his desk drawer. He was drawn to him. He wanted to help this child. He just wasn't sure how.

I first realized that Mo and I had a lot in common while both of us were looking at that photo of Kenan. "No child should have to be that strong," Mo said softly. I knew exactly what he meant. Those penetrating eyes revealed scars far more deeply than the line that ran down his cheek to his crooked smile. They seemed to be looking right into me; everything else disappeared. The depression and panic attacks, my grief and fear, all seemed to fade a little. They were still there, but knocked down a notch in the big picture of what was important. I thought I'd lost everything, but this kid . . . now, he'd really lost everything.

Mo showed me the letter from Miralem, typed in broken

print and faded ink, written on behalf of his son. What I didn't know was that the prosthetics Kenan had received in Canada two years ago were now too small and dug painfully into his skin. The letter simply read:

*My name is Kenan Malkic, I am 14 years old and have stepped on a landmine. I have no arms and a leg. I am asking all god and merciful people to help me.*

"I want to help," I said, without hesitation. And, for some reason I still can't explain, I knew I could do it. In retrospect, it occurs to me that this letter from Kenan's father was really an answer to the letter I'd written to God, asking for help in finding my way out of the darkness that was consuming my own life. It was an answered prayer.

Once I make up my mind to do something, there's no stopping me. That hasn't always been such a great thing. Selling the house I grew up in to move to Florida and marrying Bob even though I was still in love with Alfie come to mind. But when I walked out of Mo's office that day, I was filled with a powerful determination that was stronger than the fear and anxiety that had been ruling my life. I knew, without a shadow of a doubt, that this was a very good thing.

I still can't believe that within just twenty-four hours all of the roadblocks to bringing Kenan to America disappeared. I went back to work the same afternoon I met with Mo, so excited to tell my boss, Dr. Bhuphathi, who was an orthopedic surgeon, what I was trying to do. Of course he wanted to help. Not only did he volunteer to perform surgery on Kenan's leg or arms if necessary, but he called someone he knew at St. Vincent's Hospital on Staten Island to see if they'd donate physical therapy after Kenan was fitted with his new limbs. I was surprised by how quickly the hospital said yes, and that gave me the courage to call a local prosthetics company to see if they'd donate the new limbs Kenan needed. And just like that, another yes!

The airline tickets for Kenan and Aida took a bit more persistence. All of the airlines I called asked me to fax a request and wait for a reply—but I didn't have the time to wait. It seemed urgent to get Kenan here for help *now*; he'd been waiting so long without hope and I knew exactly what that felt like. I wasn't going to let him wait any longer. Period. After three or four tries with different airlines, Austrian Airlines came through with a yes in just forty-five minutes.

Now I was on a roll and I just kept on going, enlisting friends and family: My uncle Vincent, a general surgeon, offered to pay for the hotel Kenan and Aida needed to stay in for an overnight layover in Zagreb, Croatia. Rita Lu donated money to cover expenses during Kenan and Aida's stay, as did other friends and family members. I found myself at the center of something bigger than my own fears—helping another human being have a better life. It was exciting and empowering, a feeling I hadn't felt in a very long time.

That night I was blissfully exhausted, lying in bed with my big bear of a dog, Obie, sprawled out next to me. Then, little questions—okay, *big* questions—started bubbling to the surface: Where exactly were Kenan and Aida going to stay for four months? They couldn't stay at Rita Lu's. She was remodeling. There was barely enough room in my one-bedroom townhouse for Obie and me. And who was going to take them to doctor appointments, make sure they had groceries, show them around the city? Me, who gripped the steering wheel during my three-mile morning commute and couldn't drive on the highway? I didn't want my questions to turn into the anxiety I knew so well; instead, I prayed.

I'm not a very religious person. But I do have total faith in God, and I know for a fact that miracles do exist. I've learned during the past fourteen years of running this charity that nothing is a coincidence. And I knew back then, on that day in Mo's office, that God was offering me a miracle in the form of helping Kenan. To this day, I pray every night for help with specific children. Every one of the Global Medical Relief Fund kids—some who, like Kenan, survived stepping on a land mine, others who were shot by a sniper or the victim of a car bomb, and others who endured being trapped in their own home or a pile of rubble after an earthquake—are all living, breathing miracles. And I've also learned that God has a habit of answering my prayers at five minutes to midnight, just when it seems that time has run out. I guess its God's way of teaching me to have a little more patience.

The next morning, I woke up with a calm, light sensation, my heart filled with the answer to my prayer: Kenan and Aida were going to stay with me. I wasn't sure how I would make this work, but I was excited to find out.

As I held the phone to my ear, my heart was pounding—in a good way this time. "Hello?" a sweet little voice said. Mo had told me that Kenan knew some English from living in Canada, but I wasn't sure exactly how much he remembered.

"Kenan?" I asked. *How could it be him?* I wondered. *He couldn't possibly answer the phone with no hands.*

"Yes, it's me," he said. "Who is this?"

"This is Elissa," I said. "I'm the woman whose house you're going to stay at in New York. I just wanted to call and say how happy I am that you and your mom are coming here. You're going to stay with me while you get your new arms and leg."

There was dead silence. I wondered what might be going through Kenan's mind. Later, he told me that he hadn't really believed it when the woman from the Bosnian embassy called to tell his mother that I had made arrangements for him to come to New York and be fitted for new prosthetics. "Tell me, what do you want to do while you're here?" I asked, wanting to give as much as I could to this child who had lost so much.

"I want to come to New York and eat pizza, just like the Mutant Ninja Turtles," he said. We both laughed.

"Okay then," I said. "That's exactly what we'll do!"

## CHAPTER SIX

# Pizza and Ninja Turtles

*New York, November 1997*

*Breathe, breathe, breathe.* That was what was racing through my mind as I stood in the stuffy room at John F. Kennedy Airport, crowded with reporters, waiting for Kenan and Aida to get off the plane from Bosnia. It had become big news that a Staten Island medical assistant had somehow arranged for a fifteen-year-old triple amputee from a war-torn country to get new limbs, all for free.

Once I made the decision that Kenan and Aida would stay with me in my house, the *how* of it all started to unfold. A woman I worked with lent me a daybed for Aida to sleep on in my downstairs living room, and Kenan could sleep on the pull-out couch. Friends and family chipped in to create a fund to pay for groceries and whatever else my houseguests needed during their four-month stay, because they knew I had no money to spare. This act of doing something positive together reconnected me with my loved ones. I had been so disconnected for so long.

*Please, dear God, don't let them be wandering around the airport, a kid who learned some of his English watching* Teenage Mutant

Ninja Turtles *and his mother who doesn't know much more than* "hello" *and* "thank you." It had been a half hour since their plane landed, so my friend Bob, who knew people in Customs, whipped out his walkie-talkie. Within minutes he had a lead on where they were. An airline representative had been standing by at the gate with a wheelchair, ready to escort Kenan and Aida to the VIP room where we were all waiting. But when the sea of passengers deplaned, Kenan had walked right past him, unnoticed, wearing his outdated, too-small prosthetic leg and two arms. He and his mom were last seen at Immigration and could be hailing a cab by the curb at this very moment for all we knew.

While Bob went to track down Kenan and Aida, I sat in the tiny room with no windows and waited. I stayed close to the door, praying it would open soon. Praying the blonde reporter with the big hair and shoulder pads out to here would stop squeezing into my space. I stared down at my black chunky Candies to focus on something other than the impatient buzz of the reporters, trying to defuse the all too familiar fluttering in my chest. *Good Lord, why did I wear these platform shoes instead of ballet flats? They're cute, but they're killing my feet.*

It was no use. I couldn't distract myself. What had I been thinking, volunteering to take care of this boy? How would I drive him to doctor appointments and physical therapy? Me, who could barely drive to work without a panic attack.

Suddenly, all eyes were glued to the door as it swung open, letting a welcome gust of fresh air into the stuffy room.

"Here's the boy we've all been waiting for," Bob said, holding the door open. I took a deep breath and held it as Kenan walked in, a few steps behind his mother, glancing down as cameras flashed and microphones waved in his face. Reporters were shouting questions: "How does it feel to be in America? What's it like in Bosnia? Is there still shooting? Is there still tension?"

Kenan answered mostly with just a nod or a few words, looking around the room, his eyes tired but wide, as if he couldn't believe all of these people were here to talk to him. I kept thinking how much this child had seen and been through during the past five years. But it wasn't the scar running from mid-cheek to the corner of his mouth or the crooked smile that hid missing teeth—reminders of Kenan's accident—that struck me. It was his deep brown eyes; he looked wise beyond his years. Maybe that's why the reporters kept lobbing complicated political questions at him. But Kenan was obviously exhausted, and looked down at the floor—right at my chunky platform shoes.

"I like your shoes," Kenan said softly, giving me a shy smile. I let out a long breath—I knew there was some reason I had chosen these uncomfortable things! Years later, he told me that he'd been drawn to me right away because of the way I was dressed. I was wearing a crinkled rainbow-colored skirt and a turquoise peasant blouse, silver earrings dangling to my shoulders. "You had this rock star cool style," he said. "You looked so welcoming and approachable. Like someone I'd pick out to ask for directions on a crowded street."

"You have an adorable smile," I said to Kenan that day in the airport, my hand on his shoulder. "It makes me so happy." And that was the truth: I was happier than I had been in a long time.

Kenan kept glancing over at me while he was answering the

reporters' questions, as if he already knew I was a safety zone for him in this strange place with fast-talking people. And he was still looking at my shoes. It wasn't until weeks later that Kenan told me he'd become used to keeping his gaze down at floor level, focusing on people's shoes, afraid people would stare at him. That's why during the ten-hour plane ride from Bosnia to Vienna, and then on to New York after an overnight stay, he'd insisted on wearing the too-small prosthetic leg that rubbed his knee raw and the arms that pinched his elbows.

I wanted Kenan to feel special when he arrived, so we rode from the airport to Staten Island in a limousine. A kind person had paid for our ride. As Kenan stared out the window, he was awestruck. "Everything is so big," he said over and over. I pictured his view from the eyes of a fifteen-year-old boy who had grown up in a small town in Bosnia. Driving along the Belt Parkway, the lights from Coney Island took on a brighter shine, the Verrezano-Narrows Bridge that connected Brooklyn to Staten Island seemed bigger, and the Statue of Liberty glowing off in the distance was magical.

I went upstairs to change into sweats, giving Kenan and Aida a little time to unpack and get used to their new temporary home. When I came down, there was the first and only brief moment of awkwardness: Kenan had taken off his prosthetics and I could see how uncomfortable he was with me seeing him scoot around the living room on his knees. Aida asked me for ice, then she rolled up her son's pant leg. I could see there were huge red sores on his knee. "The prosthetic," she said, "it's very small."

My heart ached for him and Aida both, but I didn't want

them to feel self-conscious. "So what kind of pizza do Ninja Turtles eat?" I asked, and Kenan's face lit up.

"Pepperoni and anchovies," he said, and we all made the same disgusted face and laughed.

When the pizza came, I was amazed that Kenan could pick up a slice and eat it, using his elbows just like I used my hands. Aida later told me that he doesn't eat in front of anyone except family without his prosthetic arms, so she knew then that he was really at ease with me. It turns out I wasn't the only one who found it remarkable that Kenan could eat without using prosthetics and special silverware. A local news crew came to my house a few days later; everyone wanted to know more about this boy who had survived stepping on a land mine and was anything but crippled.

There was a cake sitting on the kitchen table and the reporter's face lit up when she saw it. "I'm sure people are curious to see how you do things we all take for granted—like eating," she said, motioning for Kenan to sit down as the cameraman came in closer. "I'll bet you'd love a piece of that chocolate cake," the reporter said. "Our viewers will love seeing how you do that without your prosthetic hands."

Kenan looked at me and I smiled encouragingly. I was so proud of him—of how *able* he was. I watched him pick up the plastic fork on the table between his elbows. "How's that cake, Kenan?" the reporter asked, shoving her microphone in his face.

"It's good," he said quietly, taking a bite. Suddenly, I was sick to my stomach, seeing how embarrassed and uncomfortable Kenan was. It hit me that he was doing this just to please me. I felt terrible—angrier at myself than I was at the reporter—as I cleared away the plate.

Later, after the news crew left, I sat down with Kenan. "I want to apologize," I said. "I shouldn't have let that happen."

"That's okay," Kenan said. But I could see from how he glanced away that it wasn't.

"You can depend on me to protect you. You're safe here. And you don't have to do anything you don't want to do."

Even though Kenan wanted to share his story, and I wanted people to know that children like Kenan were being injured by hidden land mines all over the world, I had to start saying no to reporters who asked the same questions over and over: How did your accident happen? How does it feel? What's the hardest part about being different? I could see how painful it was for Kenan to answer these questions. I felt his pain, actually, more fiercely than I'd ever felt my own pain. I could never stand up and say no in my own life, but I could do it for this boy I was growing to love.

———

Many times after Kenan went to sleep Aida and I sat at the kitchen table, drinking tea. One night we sat in silence for a long time, which wasn't unusual, but I sensed a sadness about her. I put my hand on her shoulder; she was shaking just slightly. "I'm sorry. Sometimes it's still very difficult," she said. "I try to forget, but some of what happened to my children . . . it is impossible."

I thought she was talking about Kenan, and I took her hand. "We'll make sure Kenan gets what he needs," I said softly. "We'll take care of him."

Then, Aida told me about her other son, who couldn't be saved. She cried as she quietly explained how there was no electricity to run the generator needed for the incubator when the electricity was cut off. The incubator that could have saved her premature baby. I was so honored, seeing how difficult it was for Aida to talk about Adnen, knowing this wasn't a story she told many people.

"I understand that sense of not being able to save someone you love," I told Aida. And then I trusted her with my own darkest secrets about how lost I was after Mommy died; the rash decisions and poor choices I made because I was afraid to trust love. Rita Lu and Grandma never understood that was why I pushed Alfie away. And then after Alfie died I was so overcome with grief and confused about how to cope—it's not all Bob's fault that our marriage fell apart during the honeymoon stage. I told Aida things I had explained only to my sister, and she and I became extremely connected. Though we'd known each other only a month, we were bonding over protecting her son, me saying what she didn't have the words to say. She even started calling me Kenan's American mother, an honor I didn't take lightly.

––––––

Kenan was something of a local celebrity; he was one of the first children injured in the Bosnian War to come to the United States for care and, according to his doctors in Bosnia, the most-injured survivor of a land mine accident. I had a whirlwind social schedule set up during the first few weeks after Kenan and Aida arrived, before the doctor appointments went into full swing. I was so excited to show my guests New York, and everyone wanted to meet them and do nice things for them. In retrospect, I should have taken things more slowly, but I didn't know then that Kenan was too polite to complain. He wasn't exactly quiet, but he was reserved. (Not like now, when he tells me exactly what he's thinking, even when I'd rather not hear it!)

John DePierro, the CEO of St. Vincent's Hospital, who was extremely supportive of Kenan, gave me two VIP tickets to a Knicks game at Madison Square Garden. Al, my boyfriend at the time, had offered to take Kenan. It was all very exciting: Kenan's name was up in lights, welcoming him, on a sign over the stadium entrance. At halftime some of the players had planned to give him gifts and his picture would be up on the kiosk over the basketball court. There were reporters and celebrities there, and Kenan was going to be the star of the evening. Aida and I were both surprised when Kenan and Al returned home way before halftime.

"I'm going to sleep. I don't want to talk about it," Kenan said.

"Maybe tomorrow?" I said, but Kenan didn't respond.

"He seemed happy at first," Al told me and Aida as we sat at the kitchen table. "But about a half hour after the game began, he told me he had to get out of there. The kid was freaking out, I could see it written all over his face."

"He'll be okay tomorrow," Aida said. But a few nights later things got worse.

Kenan and Aida went to sleep early, and I was upstairs in my bedroom, writing poetry in my journal with Obie sprawled out on the bed beside me as usual. Suddenly, I heard Kenan scream. I ran downstairs and he was sitting up on the sofa bed, Aida next to him with her arms around him. "I'm dying. I'm going to die. I'm dying," he kept saying in Bosnian.

"Bad dreams," Aida said, looking terrified herself. "Never before like this."

Kenan was sweating and shaky as I sat beside him. He later told me that he was seeing and feeling bits and pieces of the horrors he'd experienced during his young life: a friend who was killed by a sniper's bullet in front of his eyes, the glass wall in their apartment shattering around him as a bomb shook the floors, the tinny taste of blood in his mouth when he stepped on the land mine that left him nearly dead.

At the time, he didn't have to tell me what was happening; I knew. "You're having a panic attack," I said, rubbing his back. Then I admitted something to him that I'd been hiding from everyone for years. "I feel that way sometimes too. Just breathe; it'll pass. Just feel your mom's arms around you. She's not letting go, and neither am I." We sat there, the three of us, holding on to each other, Aida and I taking slow breaths to calm Kenan. In that moment we became not just close, but family—we all felt it. And it's been that way ever since.

———

Each day that Kenan and Aida lived with me, I felt the cracks in the protective shell I'd created easing open bit by bit. I'd been living alone for years, and it was good being forced to be around people again. The old me was starting to show up again, seeing how much she had missed by hiding out. Kenan and Aida were so genuine and full of life that it was easy to be around them—easy to trust them.

We quickly settled into a daily routine: Every morning Aida

would make a big breakfast of eggs, cheese, tomato, and toast—just like she did in Bosnia—and I'd eat it, even though I was more of a coffee-and-go type of person. Aida would clean, mend clothes, and bake bread and cookies for Kenan. At first I told her not to do housework while I was at work, but she saw how busy I was and I could see that she needed to be busy too. At night I came home and we shared a meal; either Aida would cook or I'd order out. Then after dinner we'd listen to music or watch TV—Kenan loves all kinds of movies—or Aida and I would make tea and talk at the kitchen table. She told me how difficult it had been for her in Canada, being away from her husband for eighteen months and dealing with Kenan's frustrations with physical therapy. When she came back to Bosnia again, Miralem was waiting at the airport and she walked right past him, didn't even recognize him. Aida spoke softly and her gentle brown eyes teared up; I realized how strong she'd had to be and the toll the past four years had taken on her. I had an immense amount of respect and admiration for her that grew into love.

The three of us joked a lot, about everything and nothing at all. Kenan admitted that his strategy for getting out of trouble, ever since he was young, was to make his mother laugh. He made me crack up all of the time and still does. I'd ask him to give me a hand with something and he'd lift up his arms with a sigh of mock exasperation, then break out in a grin. Or something little would happen—something silly that other people don't even find funny—and Kenan and I would look at each other and bust up laughing. Then, later in bed I'd start laughing again, thinking about what happened. Before I knew it, he'd text me from his bedroom downstairs to say he was laughing about the same thing! I've always had a good sense of humor, but Kenan taught me the healing power of laughter; he's one of the few people who can turn my worries into jokes and make me smile at the things I have no control over.

Aida's English was limited, but I quickly learned that she has a great sense of humor as well, just like her son. Even going to the grocery store was fun with her. I used to dread having a panic attack, hearing *Clean up in aisle three* over the loudspeaker—the mess being me. Kenan and Aida were the first ones I opened up to about my anxieties, and Aida would keep me busy scanning the shelves for things we needed, then tap my shoulder to show me something. She'd give me a comical perplexed look, holding up a box of Scooby Doo macaroni and cheese or a vegetable shaped like a body part, and we'd start snickering. Then a grocery clerk might walk by, looking at us warily, sending us totally over the edge. I have come to see laughter is the universal language, and I see it used all the time as the children I work with, from all over the world, join together in laughter.

———

Christmas came just a few weeks after Kenan and Aida arrived. Even though Muslim Bosnian children don't celebrate the religious aspects of the holiday, they do decorate a tree and open presents from Santa. This year, Kenan and Aida helped me to unwrap my collection of ornaments, some dating back to my childhood, and decorate a grand Douglas fir that dominated our living room. Aida and I hung gold garland on the stairs, watching Kenan fling tinsel all over the house—and Obie. She started tearing up, and I asked her what was wrong. "Not a thing," she said, shaking her head, her hand on my arm. "I haven't seen Kenan like this, so free and happy, for a long time. Being here, where people don't stare at him, and treat him like any other kid, it's good for him. He has a chance to be a child again."

On Christmas Eve, Aida made star-shaped sugar cookies and we decorated them with blue and red sprinkles. The whole house smelled warm and sweet, just as my home at 71 Major Avenue had smelled at Christmastime. We took the cookies over to Rita Lu's house, had a big dinner, and exchanged gifts with my family and friends. The whole evening was spent laughing and telling stories; I realized that in this short time Kenan and Aida had really become part of my family. And, like Kenan, I was also feeling free and happy for the first time in years.

During the Christmas season, people from all over Staten Island started reaching out to help Kenan and Aida. Neighbors brought over casseroles, movie tickets, and warm clothes for Kenan to wear now that it was beginning to snow. I felt supported in a way that I hadn't for a very long time. This wasn't a replacement for the big extended Italian family back on Major Avenue—that could never be replaced. But it was definitely when I started my new family. That family kept getting bigger and bigger—soon envelopes containing five or ten dollars, the occasional check for more—came from all over. I put the money in a bank account to pay for Kenan's follow-up visits, since I knew that he'd have to come back periodically as he grew to be refitted.

That's how the Global Medical Relief Fund started, even before it was an official charity, and that's how I've kept going ever since. Schools put on carnivals, churches have bake sales, a few neighbors have a yard sale. A kindergarten class might collect pennies in a big jar that adds up to more than $100. Back then, I wouldn't have dreamed that this new family I had created with Kenan and Aida would one day reach across the globe.

CHAPTER SEVEN

# Five Minutes to Twelve

In early March 1998, Kenan and Aida returned to Bosnia. They had been with me for four months, but it felt like a lifetime; I felt that familiar sense of loss creeping in once again. After I watched them board the plane, I went back to my house—which I considered *our* house now—and sat on the back balcony in the dark. "I miss them already," I whispered, looking up toward the stars. "And I miss you too." Even though my mother had died more than twenty years earlier, it was—and still is—a comfort to talk to her. I closed my eyes, feeling a cool spring breeze kicking up. I could practically hear Mommy cheering me on to keep going.

I lay awake in my bed for hours, dreaming up plans: Kenan was still growing and would need to come back and be refitted for new limbs in about six months, so of course I'd make that happen. And maybe I could raise enough money to bring just one more child from Bosnia here for medical care. I thought about how there were millions of children all over the world who weren't getting the medical care they needed, but somehow that wasn't a daunting thought. It only inspired me to be stronger and do whatever I needed to do to help even just a few children. The next morning, at nine sharp, I called my accountant to discuss setting up a nonprofit charity, with the intention of raising enough money to bring over another wounded child from Bosnia. At the time, I was still working a full-time job and had no intention of making a career change—especially a change to a career with no salary. George suggested a nearly perfect name for the charity: Medical Relief Fund for Children. "Global," I added. "I want to help kids all over the world." Suddenly, my dream actually had a name and became something real.

I was excited to tell Mo Sacirbey about my plan, and of course, he had an even bigger idea. He suggested that I go to Bosnia myself, visit hospitals and orphanages, and help shed a light on how many kids were injured during the war and still needed help. He had this crazy idea that the media would be interested in a medical technician/singer from Staten Island who was trying to change the world, one child at a time—and that people would listen to what I had to say.

"What makes you think I can really make a difference?" I asked quietly. Here was a man who had helped to negotiate peace talks. What the heck did he see in me?

"You have an incredible energy and spirit," Mo said. "So many people have been trying to create peace for such a long time . . . they're exhausted, burnt-out. They need someone fresh to carry on the fight. For the children—our future."

I looked into Mo's lined face: I knew he was talking about himself. How could I say no?

A few weeks later, I was going to Bosnia.

———

I landed in Sarajevo thinking that I knew a lot about Bosnia from hearing Kenan and Aida's stories about the war that had ended two years earlier. Even though they had warned me that the country was still recovering, I was still shocked to see the devastation: bombed-out buildings and torn-up streets. Everything looked gray, even when the sun was shining. In contrast, the majestic snow-capped mountains in the background were gorgeous; it was truly heartbreaking. And the people were, overall, so friendly and kind: smiling and nodding good morning as I passed on the street, shopkeepers striking up conversations in broken English. Even the cab drivers and bus drivers were friendly, playing the radio and humming along, stopping to get a coffee and asking if the passengers wanted anything. The one word that kept coming to my mind was *persistence*. The Bosnians had been through such horrors, yet they tried to be cheerful and show a reverence for life. Nearly every balcony, even on the houses with the roofs still torn off and windows blown out—had pots of sunny marigolds, lavender petunias, and bright red roses spilling over the railings. Being there truly fed my soul and gave me persistence.

I stayed with Kenan's family in their modest two-bedroom apartment in Maglaj, and from the first day I arrived it felt like home. The Malkics welcomed me with open arms, and to me their town seemed a lot like the Staten Island I had grown up in. Kenan's family was close-knit—uncles and aunts, grandparents, and cousins all living within a few blocks of each other. Suddenly, I was part of a new and wonderful second family, complete with a doting grandmother who cooked like she could have been Italian. Food and laughter are such universal languages, and we had a lot of both. Miralem, who doesn't speak much English, kept asking if I was hungry or wanted a drink.

He'd go out to the bakery on the corner after dinner and bring home a big brown bag filled with gooey surprises. Aida would make coffee and we'd sit in their living room, not talking much but just enjoying the sweets and the company.

There was so much love and joy in Kenan's family, yet I could also clearly see what a toll the war had taken on all of them. Miralem was tall and handsome with wavy brown hair and a soldier's solid stance, but his face was creased with worry and I could see the exhaustion in his eyes. Everyone in town knew me as the woman who had helped Kenan, and as Aida and I walked through town they'd all stop and bless me. Then they'd look at Kenan with such pity, saying hello in a too-sweet voice. As he glanced down, I thought of him staring at my shoes in the airport. This kid had become so confident in New York, and here he seemed to be taking giant steps back. He wouldn't even come out of his bedroom without his prosthetics on, for fear that his parents might have company over. He constantly told me how much he missed New York; I knew I had to bring him back.

During the next week Miralem took me to the country's main hospitals in Sarajevo and Zenica, as well as several orphanages in the mountains. I had expected the orphanages to be rundown, but was shocked at how dilapidated the hospitals were too: there were stains on the dingy white walls, cracked windows held together with duct tape, and windowsills with chipped paint. The electricity worked for only a few hours a day in Maglaj and not much longer in Sarajevo, the capital city. There was no air-conditioning in the hospitals, the elevators didn't work, and the operating rooms ran on emergency generators. I saw children with bandages on freshly amputated limbs that were very much in need of changing. These children were also victims of hidden land mines. The nurses told me, apologetically, that the hospital was still short on even the most basic supplies.

I carried with me a small notebook and made a long list of the children I met who needed new limbs. I kept thinking about Kenan telling me that there was no anesthesia during his surgery, and how incredibly painful that must have been for him. I kept thinking of how much pain all of these children had to be in now. There was just so much need. How could I help all of them? But even helping one child was proving nearly impossible. I spent hours talking with the hospital administrators, orphanage directors, and government officials with whom Mo had connected me. Many were suspicious of my motives: why in the world would I want to help strangers from another country? And even those who did seem to trust me weren't willing to put me in contact with the parents of the children on my list. There was no protocol for doing what I was attempting, and an insurmountable pile of red tape. One thing I learned during this experience was the art of acting more confident than I actually was. And it was amazing how, by putting on that act, I actually did become more confident. I learned to never take no for an answer and that, eventually, I'd find my way to yes.

———

Just a few days before I was set to return home, my persistence paid off: Faruk Zubčević, the news anchor at the town's only television and radio station—the Tom Brokaw of Maglaj—agreed to interview me about my mission to help wounded kids who needed prosthetic limbs. Most people in Maglaj have satellite TV, but every night everyone tunes in to watch this small man with a huge handlebar mustache on the local news. When we met at the television station, I told Faruk about my frustration dealing with hospital officials and all of the roadblocks I was encountering in trying to connect with another child who needed a prosthetic limb. A huge grin spread across his face as he nodded. "Stop your worries," he said. "It's done."

Even before the broadcast had finished, people were coming with X-rays, medical reports, and even photos of injured relatives—all of them asking me for help. Most of them were adults, and I had decided that my focus would be on helping children. The handful of kids who did come with their parents were either burn victims or had chronic illnesses, and I hated turning them away. I had the resources and know-how to help another child the same way I'd helped Kenan, but I also knew the limits of this charity I'd filed papers for just a few months earlier. I had to stick to my mission back in the beginning— helping kids who needed prosthetic limbs—or my little charity would become overwhelmed and unable to be any good to anyone—although, eventually, I did break my own rules.

After a few hours, a thin little girl in baggy overalls with dark brown hair tucked behind her ears came walking through the door on crutches. Her mother told Aida, who translated, that nine-year-old Eldina had lost her leg four years ago when a grenade exploded near a friend's backyard where she was playing.

Eldina clung to her mother's side and just stared at me with her enormous dark eyes, like she couldn't quite believe this lady dressed in faded jeans and a pink T-shirt—certainly no doctor—would be able to help her. Eldina's mother told Aida that it had taken a year for her daughter to be fitted with a prosthetic leg at the hospital in Zenica, and during the time she waited she couldn't go to school and rarely left the house because it was so hard to get around. Even after she had a new leg, she often left her classes because the ill-fitting limb was painful to wear.

I knelt in front of Eldina and smiled at her. Slowly, a grin broke over her face and that was it: she stole my heart. It was just like seeing that picture of Kenan in Mo's office that day. I knew I had to help her. Period. No matter what it took.

## CHAPTER EIGHT

# Learning Curve

🌿

🌿 There are some things that you can figure out only by taking a deep breath, jumping in, and doing; starting a charity is one of those things. GMRF became an official charity just after I went to Bosnia for the first time in early 1998, but it took nearly a year—and a steep learning curve—to bring Eldina here.

Mo had warned me that the UN Mission to Bosnia couldn't help push through the medical visas needed for Eldina and her father, Ismet, like they had done for Kenan and Aida as a favor to Mo. I thought to myself, *How hard could it be?* It turns out, it was very hard. From waking up in the middle of the night to fax the American embassy in Sarajevo because their electricity was so sporadic, to several trips for Eldina and her father over dangerous mountain roads to secure the required visas, to nearly a month's wait to get a flight booked because only one plane left Sarajevo each day, I began to see all that was required to bring just one child here for medical care.

In a happy coincidence, Kenan had outgrown his first prostheses and needed to come back to New York, so he and Miralem were able to travel with Eldina and Ismet. I now always try to have two families come together, one who's been through this process before, whenever possible. This is a life-changing trip for all of these families, most of whom don't know English and many of whom have never traveled far from the village where they live, let alone to another country. It's an exciting journey, but it can also be full of anxiety. It helps to have another family along who has done it before. These parents and children become more than friends during these trips—they become like family.

————

When I met Eldina, Ismet, Kenan, and Miralem at the gate at JFK, the first thing that struck me was how different Kenan appeared from when I had first met him, and even when I had seen him last in Bosnia a year earlier. No more staring at shoes; he looked people straight in the eye. As we went to pick up the baggage, Kenan stayed close to Eldina, explaining everything to her in Bosnian. She was so excited, looking around at the people and shops, asking questions.

Kenan's injuries had been so severe that he had received a lot of media attention when he arrived, and there were a good number of donations—money and goods—to help him. But it was different with Eldina because her case wasn't nearly as extreme as Kenan's. There was very little media attention, but luckily I had found what would wind up being an even bigger source of help.

The night before I had boarded a plane for that first trip to Bosnia I was throwing things in and out of a suitcase, worrying about what I'd wear to visit hospitals and look professional. And did I even have enough underwear for two weeks? I wasn't really worried about my clothes, though. The big question was:

How in the world would I pull off a repeat performance of how I'd helped Kenan? St. Vincent's Hospital and NovaCare had agreed to treat another child, but a part of me knew that I'd wind up wanting to help so many more.

Suddenly, my phone rang and I was surprised to see a fax scrolling in at close to midnight. I read the short note after it dropped to the floor:

*I hope you don't think I'm crazy contacting you so late. I'm a cop, I work for Crime Stoppers, so you know I'm legit. I saw you on the news tonight, talking about wanting to help kids who need prosthetic limbs. I think I can help you. Please call.*

The next morning, Joe Quinones told me he was a Shriner and that Shriners Children's Hospital in Philadelphia wanted to meet with me and discuss how they could help other children like Kenan who need prosthetics and can't get them in their own countries. I knew that Shriners was a big charity, but I had no idea how huge this offer was. All I was thinking was that maybe I could help a few more kids. I thanked Joe and told him I'd call him back after I returned from my trip. Now, with Eldina here and a list of other kids that I'd gathered during my two-week trip, I was plenty anxious to prove myself to Joe and Shriners.

During the previous six months, I had gone to a number of meetings with the administrators at Shriners Children's Hospital in Philadelphia. The hospital board was still in the process of giving my charity the green light—they wanted to make sure I could handle all of the details involved with bringing children here from another country. I tried so hard to appear confident as the board asked how I was going to care for the children I planned to bring here. Where would they stay? How would I feed them? I had some temporary options, but mostly I was making it all up as I went along. But the key was that I really did believe in myself—and I had a small but growing base of supporters, including Mo, the doctors I worked with, and people like Joe, who believed in me too. During the three months that Eldina was here, I had my chance to show Shriners that I could pull it off.

It took nearly another year of conversations to get three more Bosnian children approved by Shriners Children's Hospital for treatment, but it was worth the wait. The hospital donates prosthetics, medical visits, surgery, and physical therapy to each child they serve—it is incredibly generous. And unlike many organizations, Shriners also covers the yearly follow-up visits and new limbs needed as the children grow until age twenty-one. All I had to do was come up with the money for airfare, a place for the families to stay while they were here, and food and transportation for the one- to six-month stay each visit required. It was definitely a start.

_____

In June 1999 I went on my second trip to Bosnia. On the plane ride, I thought about how different I felt now than when I had first gone. I was calmer and more sure of myself. At the same time, I was a lot more realistic. I knew how difficult it was going to be to find children to help, especially since this time I had a specific mission to find three children—one Croatian, one Bosnian, and one Serbian. This was a symbolic gesture, but an important one to my mind and to that of my friend Boro Vuka-dinovic, who sponsored the trip, as well as part of my first visit to Bosnia. His reason for wanting to help me just blew me away: "I've never been a big fan of Tolstoy, but one story I relate to is *The Death of Ivan Ilyich*. This guy lived what looked like a fabulous life, and then, on his deathbed, just hours before he died, he finally realized he had not actually been living such a fabulous life because he had lived only for himself. That would be a nightmare: that I'd lived my life and I'd missed my destiny, my chance to help others."

Boro saw what I was trying to accomplish with starting the charity as a woman trying to fulfill her destiny. I was honored that he understood that and wanted to be part of it too. He explained to me that when his country was destroyed, he had felt a lot of shame about what had happened—especially that the children were the ones to suffer because of the stubborn stupidity of adults. His hope was that by bringing three children of different ethnic backgrounds to the United States, we could show the commonalities of the warring factions: We all bleed the same color blood. A cry for help sounds the same, no matter what language it's uttered in. And the soothing touch of a helping hand can cross language barriers, borderlines, and religious differences to heal in so many ways.

I thought Boro's idea was brilliant, but it turned out to be difficult to fulfill, more so than I had imagined. In a roundabout way, though, Kenan led me to an angel shortly after I landed in Sarajevo for the second time. Miralem picked me up from the airport, Kenan sitting next to him in the front seat with a map. I was staying in Sarajevo instead of their home in

Maglaj, closer to the hospitals and orphanages where I'd already scheduled visits. I wasn't going to take no for an answer this time; I was bound and determined to fulfill my promise to Boro to bring back three kids from different ethnic backgrounds who needed new limbs.

I had a reservation at an inn that Mo had recommended, but unfortunately—or fortunately—Kenan wasn't great with maps. We went down one winding street and up another, until I could have sworn we were just driving in circles. It was hot and we were all exhausted by the time we finally stopped at the small inn that I thought had to be the right one.

"No, I'm sorry, there's no reservation," the manager told me, checking his book.

"That can't be right . . . ," I said, reading his nametag and then giving him a pleading look. "Asko, can you double-check?" He just smiled, but oh, what a smile!

Asko watched for a few minutes as Kenan and I stood in the lobby arguing—nearly yelling and then laughing, as most of our arguments go—about which turn we should have taken. After a few minutes, Asko said quietly, looking straight at me, "I can probably find you a room."

That was it; those deep green eyes and bemused half smile spoke volumes. This guy who was twenty years younger than me literally had me at "hello."

Within an hour after I'd checked in, Asko called my room with the excuse that he figured I wouldn't know how to use the telephone—and he was right! Before hanging up, he asked if I'd like to meet for coffee. My heart was shouting, *Yes!* as I said quietly, "I could probably manage that."

That evening we talked for hours at a sidewalk café on a cobblestone street, mostly about the charity I was starting and the reason I was in Bosnia. There was something so unpretentious and sincere about Asko, the way he leaned across the table, listening and nodding as I told him I felt compelled to help heal the youngest victims of war. There were definitely sparks flying between us, right from that first night, and part of it was our shared passion for healing the children of Bosnia. "Here you are, this American woman who doesn't exactly know what she is doing—if you don't mind my saying so," Asko said. I laughed; I certainly couldn't disagree. "But you are so determined," he continued. "I admire the fire I see in your eyes. So many people are so tired from the war; it's broken their spirits as well as our country. I want to help you to give our children back their spirits, their lives."

Asko became my knight in shining armor, going with me to meet bureaucrats and be my translator, helping me to find my way around the city. At night we'd walk along the winding streets, listening to music wafting through the air from the open doors of restaurants. He listened to my frustrations, making me laugh when I needed it and giving me sound advice. We were a good team: I was passionate and stubborn; he was calm and knew how to work the system in his country—or, as it turned out, go around the system. We were falling in love, working together to accomplish something we were both passionate about, and it was a wonderful feeling. Everything seemed bright, exciting, and new with Asko. Just before I left for Bosnia, I had ended an on-and-off seventeen-year relationship that began after my brief marriage ended. I truly believe that Al loved me, and I know I loved him. But neither one of us wanted an exclusive commitment. After loving Alfie so deeply and grieving so intensely when he died, and then the catastrophe that was my first marriage, I was afraid to trust love. But Asko was so easy to trust; I started to see the possibility of long-lasting love again, for the first time in nearly twenty years.

During the previous year, Al had become increasingly jealous of the time I spent on my work. In a way, I couldn't blame him; I started thinking about Kenan and Eldina—and all of those kids in Bosnia I hadn't been able to help—when I got up in the morning and didn't stop even after I went to bed. Al started pressuring me to move in with him, and it felt like he was giving me an ultimatum: him or the charity. I chose the charity.

Since the charity is what brought Asko and me together, it wasn't going to be a source of contention for us. Instead, it strengthened our relationship to be joined together in this work. Even though he was twenty years younger than me, Asko was filled with empathy and maturity. He'd been on his own since age sixteen, and spent nearly two years as an interpreter for a general during the war. Like Kenan, he'd seen a lot that forced him to grow up fast.

My first week of meeting with hospital administrators was frustrating. They agreed to connect me with several children but also wanted me to pay for one of their doctors to accompany the children and their guardians. Asko was as frustrated as I was about this unnecessary cost to my fledgling charity. "There are so many children to help," he said one night over dinner. I was so frustrated that I could barely speak, but hopeful because I could see he was thinking. "What we need to do is get to the parents directly, without going through the hospitals, because they have so much red tape," he continued, then broke out in a huge grin. "I know one boy we can start with—tomorrow."

Asko explained to me that Miro, a fifteen-year-old boy he'd met at the video store they both frequented, had lost his legs when a land mine exploded in his family's front yard. Dada, the boy's eighteen-year-old brother, pushed Miro's wheelchair for a good mile down a dirt road from the hillside village where they lived so that they could meet Asko and me at a café. I knew as soon as I saw this boy that I had to help him. He turned out to be one of three children I came home to Staten Island with four days later. Asko was going to find more kids in need, but the hospital in Sarajevo came through with two more children I fell in love with—despite the fact that I had to pay for a doctor to accompany them. I've always regretted spending the charity's meager funds to pay for this doctor who basically did nothing but tag along on some appointments at Shriners Children's Hospital and give some minor input. From then on, I relied on Aida and Asko to find children who needed help. In the other countries where we now do outreach, I've developed relationships with doctors, aid workers, journalists, and soldiers who help me find kids in need of prosthetics. That way, I won't be forced into agreeing to things that aren't in the best interest of the children or GMRF.

When I left Bosnia after that second trip, with three children whose lives would be changed dramatically, my life was changed too. When the taxi pulled away from the inn where I'd spent ten days getting to know and love Asko, it was raining. He just stood there on the street in the rain and blew me a kiss, then waved until I was out of sight. It all seemed as if it was in slow motion—just like in a movie. As I saw him disappear in the back window, I couldn't help but be optimistic about having someone special in my life, to share my passion with again.

The day I came home, there was a letter on the floor of my office: a fax from Asko. It read, in part:

*I promise you that you will have me completely and always, you know what I mean . . . Something is happening to me, it is like some sort of storm, one great storm of feelings, winds, thunder, fire of passion, all that is mixed in one. And it makes me so happy.*

There was a picture of a circle at the bottom of the page, and underneath it Asko wrote: *I love you like this.* I knew exactly what he meant: I had the feeling our love was endless, like a circle. A circle that would never be broken, despite some hard times ahead.

## CHAPTER NINE

# Chimes in the Wind

*March 2000*

Even before the music began to play, I thought of the song that I'd written for Asko for this special day. Words I had, for so long, stopped believing that I would ever find a way to say again:

*I believe in rainbows and shooting stars at night,*
*of angels' gentle whispers that bring the morning light.*
*You're my bit of heaven, a flower from above,*
*for me to love and cherish from the garden of love.*

I glanced up at Kenan; he had also been the inspiration for this song, "Chimes in the Wind." Without him, I would not be here. Without Kenan, I wouldn't have opened myself up to life again, much less love. And without Kenan's poor sense of direction we would never have stopped at the inn where Asko was standing behind the front desk. "Don't go and start crying; your eye makeup will run and that will be the end of it," seventeen-year-old Kenan said, throwing me an arched eyebrow.

"I can't help it," I said, grinning, straightening his gray silk tie. He was so handsome in his black suit and starched white tuxedo shirt, his curls slicked down. When did the little boy I'd first met at JFK three years ago become a man?

"C'mon, Elissa, you don't want to mess up that pretty white dress, right?" he asked gently.

I nodded, smoothing down my full organza skirt. I was glad I'd chosen to wear white, even though this was my second wedding. This day was so different than when I had walked down the aisle with Bob, sobbing with grief. Today, though, my heart was overflowing with pure joy and happiness, real love. It was a new beginning, and white was exactly right for the occasion. As my song began wafting through the chapel, I deeply inhaled the bouquet of pink roses and baby's breath that I held in one hand and hooked my other hand through Kenan's arm.

"Ready?" he asked, taking a small step.

*I dance to the chimes that play in the wind,*
*the world is so alive and just begun to spin.*

"You better believe it," I said, hanging on tightly to his arm, looking toward the altar at the beautiful man in a white tuxedo who was smiling, patiently waiting for me there.

After nearly two years of faxes (Asko's emails were read by his employer) and phone calls, and a two-week visit the previous year, Asko and I were getting married. He'd come here two months ago on a fiancé visa that gave us three months to decide if we really wanted to do this. Asko knew even before he arrived that he wouldn't be returning to Sarajevo, even though he had a great job and an apartment near his family there. In fact, he had known he wanted to spend the rest of his life with me a year earlier; it took me a little longer. It's not that I didn't love Asko—I was sure of that right from the start. But remember, I'm the woman who ended a seventeen-year relationship with a man I loved because I couldn't commit to moving in with him. I'm the woman who let the love of her life go forever. This level of commitment was scary to me.

"Bosnia?" Rita Lu had said the word like I'd told her that Asko had asked me to move to Mars with him. This was about a year earlier, when I finally told her that Asko and I were in love. He didn't want to leave the country he grew up in, his career, or his tightly knit family. But I didn't want to leave my family or the charity I was building either.

"Don't worry, I'm not going—or at least I don't think I am," I said, thinking of my last conversation with Asko, the question he'd asked that I couldn't answer: *One of us has to make a big sacrifice, or this relationship isn't going to go anywhere, is it?*

My sister's face had been twisted with emotions, all that she didn't want to say. "Go ahead, you can tell me," I coaxed. "I could use some advice right now."

"Elissa, it's just that I don't want to see anybody get hurt— not you, not Asko. He's so young. And you . . ." Rita Lu shook her head. Me, I was the one who had been running scared from relationships ever since my father left Mommy. Alfie's sweet face flashed in my mind. I had never told anyone how much Asko reminded me of my first true love.

"But, Rita Lu, what if he's the one?" I had asked quietly. She reached across the kitchen table and put her hand over mine.

"Can't you just take your time and move a little slower?" Rita

Lu asked, patting my hand. "For once, can't you just dip a toe in the water instead of jumping in?"

We looked at each other, both of us smiling at a joke we'd shared since we were kids. When I was seven and my sister was eleven, Daddy had put a cement swimming pool in our back-yard. We were the first in our neighborhood to have such a luxury, and of course everyone was dying to come over and swim, even on days when it wasn't actually warm enough. One day Rita Lu and my cousin Mimi were in the kitchen, begging our mother and Aunt Mezzie to let them go swimming. "It's too cold; you'll freeze," Mommy kept insisting to a chorus of groans and "No we won't; it's plenty warm. C'mon, please?" My sister's jaw dropped as she glanced out the window, and everyone fol-lowed her gaze: There I was, floating in the pool in my purple swimsuit with the little flowered skirt, happy as a clam. I hadn't thought to ask if I could go swimming; I just jumped right on in while everyone else was debating whether or not it was too cold.

Last Christmas, during an emotional phone call when we both wound up in tears, Asko finally agreed to be the one to make a sacrifice for our love. He would move to Staten Island, and we'd try living together. It wasn't just our relationship I wanted to be sure of. Kenan was graduating from high school in June, and his parents had agreed to let their son move in with me. My friend Boro had offered to help pay for college, an opportunity that Miralem and Aida couldn't provide in Bosnia. Besides, Kenan had stayed with me three or four times by then, getting his prosthetics refitted as he grew, and he loved the ex-citement, opportunities, and constant motion of New York. He felt more comfortable here because he was just another face on the crowded streets instead of "the boy who had the horrible accident," the one everyone stared at with pity back in his hometown.

It turned out that Kenan and Asko got along famously, like brothers. They played Nintendo and watched scary movies. Asko had studied graphic design in high school, before he joined the Bosnian Army at age sixteen, and Kenan watched closely while Asko designed the first GMRF website. The two of them would tell jokes in Bosnian, and I'd be cracking up because they were laughing so hard. I'll tell you, my Bosnian became a lot better living with the two of them—it had to so that I could figure out what they were saying about me. Within two weeks it was like we'd been a family all of our lives, and Asko and I set a date to make it official.

Now, it seemed only right for Kenan to be walking me down the white-and-lavender runner we'd laid over worn brown carpet. My father reached out his fingers to briefly hold my hand as we passed where he was sitting, listening to my song.

*I sing to the sun that shines at me so bright;*
*I wake to a sweetness, a shining light.*
*You bring to me a rapture, a love I've never known,*
*you are my shelter, you are my home.*

This was so different than my last trip down the aisle. Then I'd been in a big, fancy Victorian estate filled with hundreds of people. I had spent the last few days scrubbing this tiny chapel at Mount Loretto myself. This was an old orphanage that the

Catholic archdiocese had donated for GMRF's use to convert into rooms where the kids and their guardians now stayed. The chapel was in pretty bad shape—it hadn't been used in years. But it was free, which was all we could afford. Asko and Miralem, who had come with Kenan and was staying for a few weeks, helped me clean the streaked stained glass. Rita Lu and my girlfriends dusted the pews while I vacuumed and got rid of the cobwebs that rimmed the lights on the walls.

As I walked closer and closer to the man I loved, taking in the warm smiles of my friends and family, looking at the cut flowers in vases at the ends of each pew and the light streaming through the stained glass, I felt so peaceful. Instead of sobbing, begging God to forgive me for marrying a man I didn't love, I was thanking God for giving me happiness. I hadn't had a panic attack in nearly five years; I was actually helping more and more children. And my little townhouse finally felt like a home. I felt my mother's presence that day.

> *I believe in a place where only prayers are heard,*
> *where God listens in to every prayerful word.*
> *You're my bit of heaven, a flower from above,*
> *for me to love and cherish from the garden of love.*

During the reception after the ceremony, I felt enveloped in the glow of love around me: friends and family, my new husband, and of course, Kenan. "This song is dedicated to Kenan," I said as the music began. "If it wasn't for him, I would never have met Asko and experienced the miracle of this day, of our love."

I had recorded Chrissie Hynde's classic "I'll Stand By You" a few years earlier and dedicated it to Kenan. That song was perfect for this occasion. Everyone was standing around the dance floor—well, actually, the entire room where our reception was held was the dance floor—clapping wildly as I put my arms around Kenan's shoulders and he put his hands on my waist. "Everyone's watching—make sure you don't step on my feet," Kenan whispered in my ear, his voice a bit shaky. I could tell he was making a joke because he was nervous with everyone watching. "You're doing great," I said, squeezing his shoulder as he led me slowly and gracefully in a simple waltz.

The room was thick with emotions as I looked around at Asko, my father, my sister, Miralem. Every last person in that room was tearing up, watching Kenan and me dance, listening to me sing those powerful words. I sang along to the chorus, holding Kenan tightly, glancing over to my husband, making them both a promise that I knew would last a lifetime: I'll stand by you.

## CHAPTER TEN

# The Day the World Changed

❧

❧ "Take it," Rita Lu said, sliding the check across the worn kitchen counter, then turning her attention to my two teenage nephews. "Louis, Alex, down the hatch with those eggs. I can't drive you to school this morning if you miss the bus."

"I'm not taking it," I said, stubbornly pushing the check back across the brown tiles, hunching over the Help Wanted section. I had recently been let go from my job. I half-heartedly circled two ads for receptionist positions and a part-time graphic designer position that looked promising for Asko.

My sister sat down on the stool next to me and sighed. "Elissa, you need the money—now."

I bit my lip and kept my head down, even though my sister was right. About a month earlier I'd been laid off from the doctors' office where I'd worked as a medical assistant for eleven years because they were closing the radiology department. Now, my mortgage was due—not to mention a stack of other bills—and Asko was still working part-time as a website designer. Even though I was constantly working for GMRF, I wasn't taking a penny as salary. How could I? There were more important things to do with that money.

"Let me run something by you," I said, clearing the kids' dishes off the table to help my sister. "What if I just worked at the charity for a year? I could do a big fund-raising push and really commit to taking it to the next level. My severance pay isn't a lot, but maybe along with Asko's paycheck we could get by."

The doctors had generously given me $17,000, which I had thought I'd use to start a retirement fund. But, what the heck, I wasn't planning on retiring anytime soon. "Do you think I could pull it off?" I asked, knowing my sister would be honest—and needing her approval.

Rita Lu was hustling her boys out the door, grabbing her coat, and she turned to smile at me, so proud. "Like Grandma Nellie used to say, 'When God closes a door, you just have to look for a window that's cracked open and give it a good yank.'"

"I guess the charity is my window," I said.

I tore out the ad I'd circled for Asko, then threw away the rest of the paper before heading out the door to go visit one of my kids, who had been paralyzed during an earthquake. Twelve-year-old Moises lived in a tiny village in El Salvador and had stepped in front of a boulder hurling down a hillside to protect his two sisters. The boy was discovered by a nurse from North Carolina who was volunteering as a missionary in El Salvador. Shortly after my wedding, Rebecca sent me an email explaining that Moises's family was so poor they couldn't afford a wheelchair, let alone medical care.

The boy was confined to bed, couldn't control his bowels, and had bedsores that had festered down to his bones.

I got into my car and picked up my cell to dial Asko's number and tell him about the job lead. Besides, he might want to come along to visit Moises after he came home from work. They'd become close during the two months that the boy had been recovering at St. Vincent's, getting strong enough to go to Shriners Children's Hospital in Philadelphia for physical therapy in his brand-new wheelchair. Asko had actually picked up quite a bit of Spanish and was my interpreter when Moises's mother wasn't around.

My call didn't go through, so I tried again, then once more.

I heard the phone ring inside Rita Lu's house, just as she called me from her cell. Within a few seconds I must have heard ten different phones ringing from inside different houses; it was like alarms going off.

"Elissa, something terrible has happened," Rita Lu said, her voice cracking.

"The kids?"

"No, no, they're fine, thank God. Turn on the radio. A plane crashed into the Twin Towers."

"Oh my God, what a terrible accident."

"They're saying it wasn't an accident."

I went numb inside, thinking of how many people must be injured. Dead. Then, it was like an electrical switch had been flipped and my entire body lit up with fear. Asko had taken the ferry into the city for work. He walked from the ferry right past the towers.

I was close to full panic mode. I was still in my sister's driveway, unable to even drive home, as I dialed the phone. "Kenan? Thank God you're home. Are you watching the news? Have you heard from Asko?"

"No," Kenan said flatly. "Are you coming home?"

"I can't." The truth was, I was paralyzed with fear, wondering where Asko was and if he needed me, knowing there wasn't a damn thing I could do about it if he did.

"We'll wait together," Kenan said quietly. "Lise, another plane crashed into the Pentagon and hundreds—maybe thousands— of people are dead. On the news, they're saying we're at war. Nobody knows what's going on. Everyone's scared; you should come home."

Kenan was scared. I couldn't even imagine the images this was bringing up for him. The memories.

"Okay, just let me drive down to the ferry terminal. Maybe he's there. Maybe . . ." My voice trailed off as I felt those moths flying up to the surface, making my heart pound faster and my pulse race. I hadn't felt like this in a very long time, but I re- membered the feelings like they still happened every day.

*Dear God, please don't take Asko from me, not now. I couldn't take it.* I prayed as I drove down Bay Street toward the terminal. I had to drive slowly; it was so crowded. People were walking like zombies, spilling into the streets, shell-shocked. The buses were running, but instead of route names and numbers on their signs they all read EMERGENCY or POLICE VEHICLE.

The phone rang. "Asko?" I answered without even checking the caller ID. I just knew it was him. "Where are you? Are you okay?"

"Yeah, babe. I'm at the ferry terminal." His voice sounded fuzzy, like he was very far away.

"In New York?" I asked.

"No, Staten Island."

I let out a long, shaky breath. "Thank God. Oh, Asko, thank God."

"I saw it," he said. "The plane flew right over the ferry, then into the tower. It was horrible. Smoke, flames. Then the Coast Guard horns and shouting, turning the ferry around."

"I'm coming to get you." I'd never heard Asko sound quite like this: scared and vulnerable.

"Babe, its chaos here. You'll never find me."

"Start walking down Bay Street. I'll find you."

Asko's face was white as a sheet when I saw him walking slowly on the side of the road. I honked the horn, pulled over the car, and got out to grab him. We just hung on to each other, crying. There were dozens of couples on the street, doing the same thing.

I drove to nearby Penny Beach, where I'd been probably hundreds of times since I was a little girl. My father used to take us kids there to watch fireworks over the Manhattan skyline. In later years, the Twin Towers were a majestic centerpiece that stood tall and proud above all the other buildings. Now, Asko and I stood on the boardwalk along with hundreds of others, in stunned silence. Some people were crying; others were too shocked to shed a tear. Some hung on to each other, as Asko and I did; others were standing completely alone. There seemed to be one unified murmur: "Why?"

It was a day that forever changed the view from Staten Island, just like when the wrecking ball demolished my friend Bobby's house all those years ago. Except now, the entire world was changing. And thousands more were feeling the pain of tragedy and the fear of what might come next.

## CHAPTER ELEVEN

# Opening Windows

By early 2003 I was working full-time on the charity and my days of living alone, staying by myself, were long gone—and that was a good thing. Don't get me wrong: some people choose to live by themselves and it suits them just fine. But I had done it out of fear; it never felt like a choice I had made. Now, sometimes I'd complain about not having a moment to myself, between the two men and the big bear-like Newfoundland puppy, Shilo—a surprise gift from Kenan and Asko after my first dog passed away—that shared my townhouse with me. Add to that the two or three kids at a time who were usually staying at Mount Loretto. Kenan would just shoot me an arched eyebrow whenever I started in on how I just needed some quiet, and we'd both grin. He knew me too well. I liked things just the way they were.

I did, however, like to start the day early so I could get a few peaceful hours of work done before my happy chaos kicked in. I'd get up around six, make a big pot of coffee, and sit at the desk in the corner of my bedroom, careful not to wake up Asko. My "office" had moved from my kitchen table to my garage and then to my bedroom as the charity had grown during the past few years. Behind the desk was my inspiration wall: dozens of photos of Kenan and the other thirty-five kids who were now part of GMRF. There were stacks on and around my desk, forms I needed to fill out for Shriners, visa applications, and copies of letters I'd sent requesting medical information that I needed to follow up on. A fat folder labeled WISH LIST bulged with letters from doctors and missionaries, as well as newspaper clippings, about kids who needed help that I was hoping to bring over if one grant or another came through. Another thinner folder was marked THANK YOU, with letters from people who had sent a donation or asked how they could help. (I still always follow up with a personal thank-you note.) And then, buried among all of the papers were dog biscuits and pizza crusts—gifts that Shilo liked to leave for me.

Asko was after me to find office space, but I couldn't afford to pay the rent, and besides, I liked getting up in the middle of the night and sneaking a peak at any emails that had come in. What I didn't see was that the charity wasn't just spilling over into my bedroom, it was also beginning to take over my entire life. And money was still a huge issue. I'd used up my severance pay from my job, and Asko was still working only part-time, even though he was trying to get full-time work. I was keeping the charity flying day to day on a few annual grants and a lot of juggling of bills and donations as they came in.

And yet, every morning I was excited to get out of bed and check my email. I never knew what might await, which child I might meet and want to help.

After Asko took off at around seven for his part-time job at a Web design firm and I drove Kenan to school, I started to plow through my to-do list. Each day was different, but each day involved a lot of driving: maybe going to pick up a few bags of food at a church and taking them to Mount Loretto; maybe driving a child and his parent to a doctor's appointment at Shriners in Philadelphia; maybe going to Costco to pick up some extra socks and underwear, toothbrushes and soap, shorts in the summer or a warm coat in the fall—there was always something the kids needed. And most every day I'd go out to Mount Loretto, sometimes with Asko, to take the kids and their guardians to a local park or maybe into the city for a special outing on the weekends. They all loved to take the Staten Island Ferry.

My life was busy and rich, and seemed to have found a new kind of normal. Unfortunately, the tranquility that I felt didn't last long. The entire country was still restless and afraid after 9/11, and the tension was particularly thick in New York. The shock-and-awe bombing of Baghdad was shocking but not entirely surprising. I'll never forget watching those first CNN images as it was happening: the night sky lit up with orange and purple flares, green flashing lights, billows of gray smoke over a skyline of exploding buildings.

"My God, there are people inside those buildings," I said, reading the news blurb scrolling across the bottom of the screen: UN SEC-GEN ANNAN URGES MEMBERS TO MEET HUMANITARIAN NEEDS IN IRAQ QUICKLY. I couldn't help but think of the Twin Towers attack: the photos of people jumping out of windows and the months spent digging bodies out of the rubble. The anguished sobs and angry screams of the people I stood with on the beach, watching as the Twin Towers collapsed in a plume of smoke.

I wondered how many people were trapped inside those buildings in Baghdad, which were crumbling to the ground like sand castles. Asko held my hand as we stared at the television, our faces pale. "This isn't like anything I've ever seen," he said. I imagined he was thinking of what he'd lived through during the Bosnian War. "It's like a dozen attacks rolled into one, with no warning. No time for anyone to escape."

During the next few weeks, as coalition forces moved from air strikes to ground attacks in a full-out search for Saddam Hussein and the fabled weapons of mass destruction, I was glued to CNN, anxiously watching and waiting for some good news. None came. More troops were being sent to Iraq, more innocent people were caught in the crossfire, and it didn't look like the fighting was going to end anytime soon. I needed to do *something.*

One night Asko and I were lying in bed, Shilo between us as always, and a video of a boy in a hospital bed came on the screen. He had the most beautiful thickly lashed dark eyes, and they drilled right into me. That's what I focused on, even while taking in the thick bandages wrapped around his head as well as both of his severed arms. My heart jumped into my throat as I sat up, leaning forward. This Iraqi boy had raw burns that would become scars peppering his face, the same blank look that I had first seen on Kenan's face in the photo Mo had shown me.

"What the hell happened to that kid?" Asko asked, turning up the sound.

The boy's voice was flat as he told reporters something in Arabic. "He wishes he'd died with the rest of his family," a translator said. "Put me back to sleep. I don't want to wake up again." That sounded so familiar.

The translator continued: "He says that he hopes whoever did this suffers as he is suffering, that they know what they have done to his family."

A photo flashed onto the screen: the same child, lying on a cot under a rusting metal grate, biting his lip in pain. His chest and torso were smeared with a thick white cream, but it didn't hide the weeping sores. At first I thought there was a black plastic coating on his torso; I leaned closer to the TV. "My God, that's his skin," I said, and had to look away as my stomach clenched into a knot.

I gripped Asko's hand as the newscaster told eleven-year-old Ali Abbas's story. The boy had been asleep when a missile hit his house in the village of Zafaraniya, thirty miles from Baghdad, at around midnight during one of the first coalition attacks. He remembers waking up to the sound of someone screaming his name, but he couldn't move. He was buried under the pile of rubble that had been his home. A neighbor dug him out and took him to a nearby hospital, as he slipped in and out of consciousness. Doctors said it was a miracle he survived; not only were both of his arms blown off in the explosion, but sixty percent of his body, from the chest down, was covered with third-degree burns.

Ali didn't know until days later that his pregnant mother, his father, three of his siblings, and eleven other relatives who lived in the house were all dead. He spent weeks lying on a filthy cot in a hospital that had been ransacked by mobs of looters—like every other hospital in the city—and was now under the guard of locals with guns, knives, and staves. Luckily, an Austrian reporter convinced a hospital in Kuwait with a special burn unit to admit the boy, and the U.S. military airlifted him and his uncle to a clean modern hospital just across the border, yet a world away.

When the CNN report was over, Asko clicked off the TV. We both sat still, somberly staring at the screen. His arm was taut around my shoulder, and I could feel the same tension in him that was surging through my body. I wasn't crying anymore; now I was getting angry. This innocent boy and his family had nothing to do with the politics that started the war and destroyed his life. As Boro often said, adults start wars over power and greed, and children are the ones to suffer.

I turned to Asko. "Are you thinking what I'm thinking?"

"Yes. Let's see if we can help him." Asko jumped out of bed and turned on the computer. We found several more heartbreaking stories about Ali. Samia Nakhoul, the Gulf bureau chief for Reuters, described in London's *The Guardian* how she'd asked a nurse at the Baghdad hospital, "What's the worst case you've received?" The nurse led the reporter into a side room, eerily silent in contrast to the noise and commotion in the rest of the hospital. Inside there was a single low bed where Ali was lying. "I have covered the Lebanon War, but I had never seen anything like that," said Nakhoul, who learned Ali's story from the woman sitting on the edge of his bed, an aunt who had stayed with him in the hospital, sleeping on the floor by his bedside, since the bombing.

"Will you help me get my arms back?" Ali had reportedly begged Nakhoul. "If I don't get my arms back, I will commit suicide." The reporter left the room and sobbed for hours, like she'd never sobbed before.

It didn't take long for Asko to find the phone number for the hospital in Kuwait where Ali was staying. "What time is it over there now?" I asked, getting excited. A few more clicks of the mouse and we found out it was seven hours later: seven thirty in the morning. I dialed the phone number and took a deep breath, looking at the photo of Kenan graduating from high school that hangs on the wall behind my desk. "Okay, here goes," I said, hearing the phone ring halfway across the globe. And miraculously, someone answered the phone and the little prayer I was silently saying.

———

"Don't get up. I'll make coffee," Kenan's voice boomed up the stairs the next morning. But I was already awake, sitting at my desk, so wired I didn't even need my morning fix of caffeine. I still couldn't believe that I'd actually gotten through to Ali's doctor, Imad Najada, at Saud A. Albabtain Center for Burns and Plastic Surgery in Kuwait City. He was thrilled when I explained that my charity works with Shriners and we could give Ali prosthetics as well as physical therapy when he was well enough to travel. Now, I was online reading more stories about Ali—there were dozens of them. Four British tabloids were raising money for him, as well as Sweden, the queen of Jordan . . . hundreds of thousands of dollars had been raised for Ali by dozens of charities. I started wondering if maybe I shouldn't try to help another child instead.

Kenan came upstairs with a cup of coffee for me, balanced between his forearms, and looked over my shoulder at a photo of the boy with a scarred face and thickly lashed dark eyes. "Who is that?" he asked, setting the coffee on the table and deftly maneuvering the mouse to scroll down the page to read the article.

"This boy is the same age you were when you had your accident," I said. "He's lucky. He's got all of these people who want to give him a new place to live, pay for his school and medical care."

"They can't really help him," Kenan said quietly when he finished reading the article. "Nobody who hasn't gone through this knows what it's like."

"You know, that's true." I thought about the stories of how Kenan had butted heads with the therapists in Canada who wanted him to use hooks for hands and special gadgets he didn't need because he could do so many things with his severed forearms.

"Elissa?" Kenan said, his voice shaky as he finished reading the article.

"What is it?"

"I can help this kid. I'll write him a letter, telling him what I can do. Better yet, I'll make a video so that he can actually see it's not hopeless. He can have a good life, even without his arms."

Asko, who had been in the shower, was now digging around in the closet. "Kenan, you're a genius," he said, pulling out a camcorder and turning it on. "Hold up that coffee mug and tell how you made the coffee," he said. "Have you brushed your teeth yet? We can film that, and then maybe you taking Shilo for a walk."

Kenan batted away the camera, laughing, and said something in Bosnian that roughly translated to: "Wait till I comb my hair at least, for crying out loud!"

"Don't worry, Kenan, you're pretty enough," Asko joked. "We have to get this tape made and in the mail."

"I'll do you both one better," I said, now certain we could help Ali in a way that nobody else could. "How about if I take Ali the video in person?"

The words just came out of my mouth. GMRF didn't have the money to pay for a trip to Kuwait, and I had just about enough in my bank account to cover a cab ride to the airport. After they both left for school and work, I called Boro, thinking maybe he could help me with a fund-raiser. He'd seen a newspaper story about Ali just that morning in *The Los Angeles Times* and was so proud of Kenan that he offered to pay for the entire trip.

A few weeks later, Asko and I were boarding a plane to Kuwait to deliver to Ali Kenan's tape and a Nintendo Game Boy. Kenan had bought this as a gift for the boy. The tape was amazing: Asko had filmed Kenan getting dressed, brushing his teeth, playing video games, playing soccer, typing on the computer, and much more, with and without his prosthetics.

———

From the first moment we arrived in Kuwait City, I couldn't help but compare the oil-rich, almost sterile, busy metropolitan environment to the slow old-world charm of Sarajevo's cobblestone streets and flowering balconies. I'd felt immediately welcome and at home in Bosnia, whereas I felt like an outsider for the entire month that Asko and I wound up staying in Kuwait

City. The people in Kuwait were friendly and courteous, but they also kept me at arm's length. The culture is very formal; women don't even touch men they aren't related to, let alone hug and kiss like the Bosnians and the Italians I grew up with in my Staten Island neighborhood.

Our cab from the Kuwait Airport headed out on an eight-lane highway, alongside Porsches, Aston Martins, and Jaguars. It was a short ride into the heart of Kuwait City, with street signs in Arabic and English, sleek glass-and-metal office buildings, and boulevards lined with palm trees. People from India, Indonesia, and Africa go there to work for the wealthy Kuwaiti business owners who made their money during the oil boom of the past seventy years. And yet, there are many signs that this is still a traditional Arab country. Many women still wear the traditional dress of an *abaya*, a head-to-toe silky black cloak, or a *jilbab* robe with a headscarf—even in the 120-degree heat of summer.

The next morning we went to the hospital to meet Ali Abbas and deliver Kenan's gifts at the time we'd set up with his physician. The hospital, just like the rest of the city, was immaculately clean. It was also surprisingly calm and uncrowded, considering there was a war zone less than two hours away. To tell the truth, it reminded me more of a hotel than any hospital I'd ever been in. Ali's private room looked like digs for a prince—complete with people waiting to see him. The room was filled with flowers and cards, teddy bears sitting up against the wall, and balloons bobbing on the ceiling. His uncle Mohammed was in a chair next to Ali's bed, and he stood and bowed when the doctor introduced us. I cringed as I heard Mohammed ask the doctor, "American?" He said it like it was a bitter taste in his mouth. Ali just looked at us with no emotion and didn't say a word. But I could imagine what he must be thinking: these are the same people who killed my family.

"We're here to help," I said, but I felt so inadequate. I couldn't bring this kid's family back. And I wasn't at all sure I could soften the hardness in his eyes. A petite Kuwaiti woman with fair skin and fine features introduced herself as Ali's physical therapist. She had a lilting Arabic accent. Nafisah translated what I was saying, smiling encouragingly at me. "There's a boy who lives with me, he's like my son, and he has no arms," I continued haltingly. "Kenan made a tape to show you what he can do. To show what *you* can do."

Ali was still just staring at me as I put the tape in the VCR. Then, as he watched Kenan getting dressed, brushing his teeth, and washing his face, his face softened. He leaned forward, his eyes wide when he saw Kenan playing Nintendo, maneuvering the joystick with what was left of his arms as naturally as if he'd had hands. "Yes! My car won," Kenan cheered, smiling broadly at the camera that Asko held. Ali actually sounded excited as he said something to Nafisah. "He wants to know if he can do that," she said, her voice brimming with hope. I gave him the Game Boy, nodding.

"See how this boy has taught himself to play this?" I asked. "With practice, so could you. In fact, you can learn to do a lot." Then, an amazing thing happened: Ali smiled at me.

"He asks, how did it happen?" Nafisah said, and I explained that Kenan had been playing soccer and stepped on a land mine almost ten years ago. I sat on the edge of Ali's bed and looked into his eyes, channeling Kenan's determination. I pointed to the television screen, where Kenan was making himself a sandwich, opening the fridge and taking out mustard and turkey, then putting bread in the toaster. "You can do that. You can learn to do a lot—just like Kenan."

"This is the happiest I've seen him," Nafisah said to me as she rewound the tape for the boy to watch again, at his request. "He says he wants to learn like your Kenan did. Other people have come and shown him prosthetics, but you came and showed him what he can do."

Sure enough, Kenan was right. Only someone who had gone through the horror of losing his arms could really understand how to help Ali. "And this isn't the half of it," I said, bursting with pride. "I wouldn't be surprised if Kenan has Ali riding a bike, and eventually driving a car!"

The doctor told us it was going to take Ali's uncle a few days to sift through all of the offers from various charities and figure out what was best for the boy. Now, we just had to wait. "We've already done what we came here to do," I said to Asko as we kicked off our shoes back at the hotel and flopped down on the bed, the jet lag kicking into full gear. "I can't wait to tell Boro and Kenan about the look on that kid's face while he was watching the video. We did a good thing coming here, right?"

"Just imagine when he actually meets Kenan," Asko said, and gave me a huge bear hug.

Not long after we fell asleep, the phone rang. It was a reporter from a British radio station. Apparently, I was the only representative from an American charity who'd offered to help Ali, and that was newsworthy. "Sure, go ahead and ask me whatever you want," I said, still half-asleep. But I snapped to fully awake pretty quickly.

"All right then, Ms. Montanti," he said in a crisp British accent. "What makes you think you can help Ali, or that he wants to be helped by Americans?"

At first I was blown away. I tried to tell him about my charity and working with Shriners, but that's not what he wanted to hear. "Are you offering to help out of guilt?" he asked. "Is this some political mission or a publicity stunt—an American offering to help a Muslim?"

"Look, we're not here for some publicity stunt," I said, gripping the phone and Asko's hand. "We're just offering help. And as for helping a Muslim, both my husband and the triple-amputee who's been like a son to me, living in my house for the past two years, are Muslim."

Silence. "Hello?" I asked, thinking maybe the connection was dead.

"Yes, well, thank you, Ms. Montanti," the reporter said, which I took as something of an apology. "I think that concludes our interview."

I thought that was the end of it, but it turned out to be just the beginning of a very long afternoon. So much for that nap I so desperately needed. I was so upset that Asko suggested a walk on the beach near our hotel. It was well over a hundred degrees and the sun was high in the sky. I was aching to at least roll up the sleeves of my long shirt and tie my ankle-length skirt into a knot at my knees. "That's all we need, you getting arrested for indecent exposure," Asko joked, reminding me that women are allowed to show skin only at private single-sex beaches. So, instead, we just sat by the water, threw caution to the wind, and took our shoes off to dip our toes into the waves.

Suddenly, a big grin spread across my face. "What?" Asko asked.

"I was just thinking what a great place this would be to set up a hot dog stand," I said. "No competition, right?"

Asko just looked at me for a minute, as if I was crazy, then shook his head. It had clicked that I was talking about my days at Smyrna Beach in Florida. "Only this time, no giving away," he said. "These people can afford to pay!"

When we returned to the hotel a few hours later, there were more than a dozen phone messages. Apparently, the British radio interview had been aired live without my knowledge. The story was already over the Internet: NEW YORK WOMAN TRIES TO PUT GOOD FACE ON U.S. ATROCITY. They even dubbed me the Wicked Witch of the West. There were calls from other reporters, as well as anonymous messages from people telling me to go home, Americans had done too much damage to this boy's life to even try to make it right. Part of me wanted to laugh, it was all so ludicrous. A bigger part of me wanted to cry.

"This isn't about politics," I tried explaining to another British reporter I called back. "It's about helping kids—pure and simple."

"But surely you must feel some responsibility," he persisted.

"For what happened, no. To help, of course. That's what my charity does."

Now, I was really crying. I was so tired, and this conversation seemed so futile. Even coming here seemed futile. Asko touched my arm. "Hang up," he whispered. "You don't need to do this. It's not why we're here."

Of course, Asko was right. We went back to the hospital to say good-bye to Ali Abbas, giving his uncle our contact information. "If he ever needs us . . . ," I said, but I knew he had plenty of help. (A nonprofit organization in London provided his prosthetic limbs and rehabilitation, and then a generous benefactor paid for him to attend private high school.) What I really wanted was to find the kids who didn't have stuffed animals lining their walls and charities lined up in the hall to see them. I found Nafisah in the hall and asked if she'd help us with that.

"I want to find children who don't have anyone else. That's why I started this charity," I said. "Will you help us to go where there's really a need? Will you help us go to Iraq?"

## CHAPTER TWELVE

# Into Iraq

🌿

🌿 I was too excited about where we were going to be scared, sitting in the back seat of a jeep with Asko, holding on to the seat in front of us and settling into the rhythm of the bumpy ride. I still couldn't believe that Nafisah had worked so quickly. In just a few hours I would be in Basra, where we would be touring hospitals the next day. It had taken two weeks of trips to the American embassy in Kuwait to get our visa and several meetings with our travel companions to plan this trip. Sitting next to us were two executives from a prosthetics company in Kuwait, who had told us that prosthetics simply weren't available in Iraq, even before the war began. Their company was small, but they wanted to see if they could donate some artificial limbs to hospitals in Basra. The problem Nafisah predicted was that there were few doctors in Iraq who had the skills to fit prosthetic limbs, let alone physical therapists. I didn't understand why we couldn't just bring more injured children to Kuwait, like Ali Abbas, but that didn't seem to be an option for reasons I could never understand.

A British soldier sat in the front seat next to our driver, Mohammed al-Saffar. Mohammed was an official with the newly formed Humanitarian Operations Center (HOC), a nonprofit group of U.S. Army civil affairs soldiers and Kuwaiti health officials who worked with the Iraqi Ministry of Health to get Iraqi children medical treatment outside of the country. He was a friend of Nafisah's and thrilled to hear that GMRF could actually bring children to the United States for medical attention. At the time, I had no idea how difficult this would actually be to pull off.

"We're approaching the border. We'd better stop for gas and take care of a few things," Mohammed said, and I gripped Asko's knee. Mohammed pulled our vehicle into a lot with two gas pumps, and we waited in line behind other military jeeps—no civilian cars were this close to the border. The soldier took a screwdriver out of the glove compartment and got out of the car. "What's he doing?" I asked, hoping he was going to pop the hood and tighten something that would crank up the air conditioner. We'd already had to turn our jeep around twice because the AC didn't work right, exchanging it for another jeep. This vehicle didn't feel all that much cooler.

"He's taking off the license plates," Mohammed answered, as if that was all the explanation needed. I looked at Asko, sitting next to me in the backseat, and he shrugged.

"Isn't that illegal, driving without plates?" I asked.

"Well, it's better than the alternative. We could get stoned—or worse—driving into Iraq with Kuwait plates. The Kuwait-Iraq war was more than a decade ago, but the hatred still remains. And aiding the British and now the Americans certainly doesn't help." This is when it really hit me what I was doing: I was an unarmed American woman going into Iraq. We were traveling on the same road used by U.S. and British Army trucks, heading to Iraq from Kuwait City, where they refueled and restocked supplies.

"Are you scared?" I whispered to Asko as we neared the border checkpoint.

"A little, but more excited. You?"

"Definitely more excited," I said. "This feels really important, like the first time I went to Bosnia." I put my hand to the silver necklace with pink rosary beads I wore around my neck. These beads were from my mother's rosary, the same one she kept on her bedside table during the years she was ill. I prayed now, my fingers on Mommy's beads, for the children I knew we'd be meeting in just a few hours. I prayed I really would be able to help them.

———

Crossing the border into Iraq was actually easier and quicker than I had expected. A Kuwaiti soldier asked us where we were going and why, and then warned us to be careful of snakes as he stamped our passports. Snakes? It struck me as odd that he didn't warn us about land mines or snipers.

As we drove on, it was like entering another world. The air was brown and hazy with sand, and the surroundings were like a moonscape: flat and dry, with scraps of brown shrubs occasionally tumbling across the highway. "There's a sandstorm brewing. We'd better hurry and get to Basra while we can still see," our driver said, and I noticed that even the air in the car seemed dry and dusty. Was the AC working at all? I didn't feel it, but I didn't want to ask; there was no turning back now.

Not far from the highway, a group of about a dozen camels

appeared as if by magic. They blended in nearly perfectly with the swirling clouds of sand. A man in a long white robe and red-checkered head scarf wrapped over his face appeared, bending deeply into the wind as he walked. "Where will he go during the sandstorm?" I asked.

"The Bedouin nomads have been living in the desert for centuries," Mohammed said. "His home is a tent packed on the back of one of those camels and he'll pitch it when the storm gets bad enough. It is such a shame that the oil fields and the fighting over that oil has changed their peaceful lifestyle. The desert is no longer safe for their families. Many live in horrible slums in the cities now."

"Wait, stop!" I couldn't be sure, but I thought I saw something—or someone—atop one of the camels, bent over the camel's neck. "Someone might need help."

Maybe it was just my imagination, the growing reality of what was to meet us in Basra playing with my mind. But I'll never know.

"We can't stop; it's too dangerous," Mohammed said, and then as if to prove his point I heard the popping sound of gunshots in the distance. I turned to look out the back window, but the camels and the nomad were now just dots moving out into the desert.

The jeep moved slowly, and sand was flying against the window; I could feel the grit in my mouth and on my skin, even though I knew the windows were sealed tightly. Actually, that thought was far from comforting; there didn't seem to be enough air in the car for all of us and I was woozy from taking Dramamine for motion sickness. Asko could tell I wasn't doing so well and put his arm around me, drawing me close. "Just close your eyes for a few minutes," he said. "You want to be rested when we get to the hospitals."

He was right, and I did rest, but not for long. Suddenly, there was a series of loud explosions, and I could hear Asko's heart quicken as he held me closer. In the distance, even through the sandstorm, I saw blazing orange, like pieces of the sun had fallen from the sky. I assumed from the smoke that the nearby oil field had recently been bombed. My first thought was to look out the back window, as if I might see the Bedouin nomad and his camels and know they were safe. Then, I pulled out my cell phone.

"Who are you calling?" Asko asked, but I didn't answer. The phone was ringing and I needed to hear the voice on the other end. Looking out at that burning oil field, I was scared.

"Daddy? It's me. I just wanted to tell you that I love you." I hadn't told my father I was going to Iraq, but I told him now. I told him how small I felt in the gigantic scope of this war I didn't totally understand. Was it about finding weapons of mass destruction? Was it about oil? Was it about 9/11? For me, it didn't really matter. It was about bringing hope to families who had gotten caught in the crossfire of a war they had nothing to do with, giving children back their lives.

"Elissa, sweetheart, I'm so proud of you, and your mother would be too," my father said. I shut my eyes and cringed against another round of loud blasts in the air. Now, Asko was calling his father also, talking to him in Bosnian. His voice was low and calm—too calm. That's how I knew he was unnerved.

"My father thinks we're crazy," he said after he hung up.

"There have been kidnappings on the news, Iraqi insurgents taking American soldiers hostage."

"Do you want to turn back?" Mohammed said. Now, there were people walking along the road with their belongings on their back, some with a donkey pulling a cart that held a few pieces of furniture, a rug, some pots and pans, and clothing, all piled together as if packed in a hurry. Small children rode on the backs of wagons, or atop the donkeys. In the distance, clouds of smoke were rising; entire villages had been burned to the ground.

"I think we're past the point of turning back," I said, wondering where all of these families—suddenly nomads caught in a war zone—were going.

The air in the jeep was thick with dust and tension by the time the city of Basra sprawled out in front of us. The sandstorm had subsided, so I rolled down the window, thinking that surely the air must be cooler outside than it was in the jeep. Boy, was I wrong: a blast of hot air hit my face. I kept the window down anyway, trying to discreetly trickle water over my head, to see this city that I'd read was the Big Easy of the Middle East. I'd done some research online and found photos of the beautiful white stone canals and bustling market bazaars that filled Basra. In older sections of the city, big houses with intricately carved wooden facades that rivaled the Victorian mansions of the French Quarter lined the streets. Basra is a commercial waterway—located at the crossroads of the Tigris and Euphrates rivers—and people have traditionally come here for good food, music, and trading. Now, though, the main streets of Basra were nearly deserted. We drove slowly, maneuvering around huge potholes and blocks of sidewalk that had been blasted into the street. Some of the shops were empty shells; others were completely demolished.

As we drove farther into town, there were scattered signs of life—and death. A woman sat by the side of the road, her head in her hands, two children huddled to one side of her and a man's body, facedown, on the other side. We passed an old American-style sedan moving slowly down the street, a plywood box strapped to the top. People walked on either side, sobbing and banging their hands against the car, as they prepared to bury a loved one. We turned off the main street, into what must have been a residential neighborhood, to see women and children sitting outside piles of rubble that had once been their homes. I wondered where the men were. Looking for food? Trying to find a safe place to take their families, a bed for their children to sleep in?

The jeep suddenly screeched to a halt, and Asko put his arm protectively in front of me so I wouldn't slam into the front seat. In the street lay two tan dogs, so thin I could count their ribs. They were curled together in a ball, and one looked up at the jeep, too weak to rise. I got out of the car with my water bottle and knelt next to the dogs to cup my hand and give them a drink. "Elissa, it's no good," Mohammed said. "Let them die sooner rather than later. What little you can help is not enough." I let the dogs drink from my hands until the water was gone, sweat trickling down my forehead, my own throat parched. I knew Mohammed was right, but it seemed important to give these animals a bit of comfort. It was an act of faith. I prayed that Mohammed wouldn't be right, that when we got to the hospital what I had to offer would be something significant, even if it wasn't nearly enough.

———

A young Iraqi doctor met us at the front doors of the Basra General Hospital, offering his hand, thanking us for coming. *A good sign*, I thought.

"Call me Doctor Ahmed," he said, putting his hand to his chest and bowing slightly. This is a sign of humble respect in Iraq, and I returned the gesture. "Mohammed has told me about your work. We are all so honored you are here to help our children."

"I'm honored to be able to offer help," I said, letting out a long sigh that held the tension of our trip. This guy was actually glad to see us! There was none of the suspicion or resistance I'd encountered in Bosnia and Kuwait.

"Come, we've told people you are coming and they wait for you," Dr. Ahmed said, leading us through the front door.

"Patients?" I said in surprise. I'd had to beg to see patients in Bosnia.

"I must warn you, even before the war, our hospital was nothing like what you have in America. Now, things are very difficult. Our supplies are low, and the main water line was severely damaged in the bombing."

Having worked in hospitals for more than twenty years, I wondered how this one could function without water. "A truck brings water to us twice a day," Ahmed said, reading the question on my face. "But we must use it sparingly. It is never enough . . ."

The doctor's voice trailed off as we saw women in long black robes and head scarves sitting on blankets, some with small children, lined up against the walls of the entry lobby. The floors and walls were coated with a thin layer of gray dust that wafted through the open windows even though the air was perfectly still. "They stay here, waiting to see loved ones who may be in surgery or perhaps sleeping," Ahmed said wearily. "They have nowhere else to go. And more keep coming every day."

I reached into my big black purse, my fingers grasping for something I could give these children who smiled shyly as we passed. Why hadn't I thought to bring . . . what? I couldn't think of anything I could have brought that would be even close to adequate.

"No electricity," Ahmed said, like he was apologizing, as we walked down a dark corridor. I had to put my hand to my nose: the air was heavy and the smell was wretched—like death. Asko took my other hand and squeezed it briefly; it was too hot for anything more.

I wasn't prepared for the scene that greeted me when we entered a room toward the end of the hallway: at least fifty people, mostly women, were waiting inside, armed with X-rays and medical records. They were standing, waiting, smiling, and bowing. "*Shokran jazeelan, alhumdulilah,*" they said over and over. "Thank you, God bless."

Dr. Ahmed had a table set up for me, and people lined up to show me their medical files and tell their stories. They looked into my eyes, some speaking in low, shaky voices and others in sharp, urgent tones. Of course, I didn't need to know Arabic to understand what they were saying.

Mohammed translated. "This one says her daughter has been in the hospital for a month, and now they must let her go even though she has lost both arms. She also has trouble breathing, maybe from chemicals."

The woman was crying, begging me with such pain in her eyes that I teared up too. "She asks, who will marry my daughter now?" Mohammed said softly. "Who will take care of her?"

I had no answer for this woman. I had no answer for the mother who asked how her son, who had lost his leg and his feeling from the waist down, would make a living. I had no answers for any of them. "I don't know if I can help, but I'll try," I kept saying. "Please know that I care, I want to help." The Iraqi people were so warm, so grateful that I cared enough to visit. I wanted to give them hope, but at the same time I didn't want to make any promises I wasn't sure I could keep. My partner, Shriners Children's Hospital in Philadelphia, was world renowned for pediatric orthopedics, but that specialization was also limiting for me. It would be years until I also partnered with a group of plastic surgeons who would expand the help I could offer children who were badly burned from land mines, as most of these kids were. Still, I kept writing down names on my yellow legal pad. There was nothing else I could do. I touched the pink rosary beads around my neck—hidden beneath my shirt, at Mohammed al-Saffar's suggestion—and silently prayed that I could make even a small dent in this madness.

It took me three hours to talk with every last parent in that room, and I had a list with dozens of names on it as well as medical files. "Would you like to meet the children?" Dr. Ahmed asked.

I wasn't expecting the hotel-style luxury of Ali Abbas's room in Kuwait City, but neither was I expecting the scene that met me next: A room with hundreds of injured children, from toddlers to teenagers—most with burns on their faces and arms, some missing a limb—lying on rows of cots. The floor was a maze of people sitting, or curled up trying to sleep, some sitting on the edge of a bed and trying to comfort a crying child. Dr. Ahmed led us around to the children whose mothers we'd met in the other room, and Asko took photos. I walked from bed to bed, leaning closer to smile at each child, and look past the bandages and fresh pink scars. At first, most of their eyes appeared blank with shock. But as I leaned closer I could see the terror, the same fear I'd seen in Kenan's face the night of his panic attack.

It was an exhausting, draining feeling, one I still experience too often even today, that knowledge that I can never really do enough to heal all of the world's wounded children. Who can? Sometimes I forget that it's not just about what I'm doing, but the cumulative efforts of us all, the positive force that's created through a worldwide network of helping one child at a time.

———

"How was it for you, after everything you went through in Bosnia?" I asked Asko that night at dinner. Mohammed had taken us out for an early meal back in Kuwait. The day that had just passed felt like a dream, unreal. I sat gazing out of the floor-to-ceiling windows at a gorgeous view of the Kuwait City skyline. Beyond that, the sun sat blazing pink and orange as it set over the ocean. I was fascinated by how my water glass was constantly refilled after spending the day in a hospital where water was a precious commodity.

Asko blew out a long breath and shook his head. "There's no comparison," he said. "In Bosnia, I knew what to expect because it was conventional warfare. The military maneuvers all happened at the front line, and for the most part, the other towns didn't experience big attacks. People were afraid of snipers or an occasional rocket shelling, but it was nothing like the chaos in Iraq. The whole idea of shock-and-awe is that your enemy can be anywhere and attack at any time."

"And kill or maim anyone, at any time," I said softly, thinking of the children I had met in Basra.

I stabbed my fork into my salad and moved the lettuce and bits of tomatoes around. I hadn't eaten since breakfast, but I wasn't hungry. I took my yellow legal pad out of my purse and put little stars by a few names. "Even if we can only bring one or two kids back to the States with us . . . that's a start," I said. "What if we went back one more day? Didn't Ahmed say there's another hospital we could visit?"

"Elissa, what you did today is a wonderful thing," Mohammed said. I didn't like the tone of his voice, like a pat on the back that implied there was nothing more I could do. "As you know, our organization has placed children in Great Britain, Australia, and Europe, but never the United States," he continued. "I'm not at all sure you can get visas for Iraqis."

"That can't be right," I said, cutting him off, not wanting to hear him tell me what I couldn't do. I only wanted to know what I *could* do.

———

A few days later, Asko, Mohammed, and I were on our way back to Basra, to visit one final hospital. This time we knew what to expect. This time, we had a plan. Mohammed suggested that we look for just one child who needed a prosthetic limb and no other care, someone who could easily travel back to the United States with us, along with a guardian, on a commercial flight. I was giving up on the other kids on my list, but I agreed what I really needed right now was to find one child with a fairly simple case who might open the door for other children who had more complicated situations.

We left before the sun had even come up, so we would have the whole day. I was terrified of being trapped in Iraq overnight when the border closed in the early evening. Luckily, we made it to the hospital by mid-morning—without air-conditioning troubles or sandstorms this time. The hospital was much like the other two, but I didn't feel so bleak walking through the corridors. I had a plan.

"This is it. Are you ready?" Dr. Ahmed asked, his hand on the doorknob to the room where wounded children were waiting. I nodded, bracing myself as he opened the door. Immediately, I heard something that made me look through the crowd of people around me. It was a child's voice, yelling something in Arabic to get my attention. A beautiful boy with jet-black hair and matching eyes smiled at me from across the room and raised a bandaged arm without a hand.

I waved back to the boy, feeling those familiar wings fluttering in my chest, the excitement of knowing something good was about to happen. I was going to help this kid, smiling at me as if he had been waiting for me to arrive. How could I not?

I went over and sat on the edge of the boy's bed, pointing to myself. "Elissa," I said.

He sat up straight and smiled at me, taking my hand to put it on his chest. "Ali," he said. We sat there smiling at each other, my hand feeling his heart beating. It was as if he was telling me that he was putting his life in my hands.

I reached out to touch the boy's bandaged arm, remembering how much Kenan appreciates it when people make physical contact with his forearms, instead of shying away, if he's not wearing his prosthetics.

I pulled out my photo album from my purse and Ali moved closer to see the first photo of me, Kenan, and my dog. "Shilo," I said, pointing to the dog. "Woof, woof." Ali tilted his head back and let out a wolf-like howl, then laughed. I pointed to Kenan. "My son," I said. "He lost his arms in a war, like you." Mohammed translated for me as we went through the pages, me talking in English and Ali in Arabic. But we didn't really need words. When I came to a photo of Kenan where Ali could clearly see he was wearing prosthetic arms, his face lit up and he pointed to himself.

"Yes, you, I promise," I said, and Ali hugged me as if to seal the deal.

## CHAPTER THIRTEEN

# Keeping My Promise

Adults make lots of promises, and, as adults, we've learned to take what people say with a grain or two of salt. *I promise* usually translates into *I'll try.* Or, sometimes it just means *Quit bugging me. End of discussion.* But when I give my word to a child, I take that responsibility very seriously because I know they believe what I've told them. They're counting on me. They trust me. And when a child has all that faith in what you're telling them, when they're counting on you to give them back their life, breaking your promise is much worse than never having made it in the first place. Keeping the promise I made to Ali Ameer in that hospital in Basra wound up being one of the most difficult things I've ever done. It took over my life—my marriage, my job, my waking and sleeping hours—for an entire year.

I knew I was in trouble right from the start, when I went to the American embassy in Kuwait after returning from Basra. I had Ali's medical records, which I needed to get approval from Shriners, and I knew that Ali's aunt Narges, an elementary school teacher I met briefly at the hospital, was willing to travel with him to the United States for his new hand. Narges, a sweet, quiet woman in her early thirties, told me that Ali's family lived just down the street from her. The boy's mother was pregnant with her seventh child, and he'd been living with Narges for several years. Asko and I waited in line at the embassy, baking in the hot sun for three hours only to be told that getting visas for any Iraqis to travel to the United States was flat-out impossible. "You don't understand," I said to the clerk, certain that I could make him understand. "This is a medical visa I'm talking about. For a child who's an innocent victim of the war. They're going to other countries; why not ours?"

"You're facing several problems," the clerk explained. "First, there's no government in Iraq, which means there's no office to process passports."

"So how do Iraqis get visas with a passport?" I asked, cutting to the chase.

"They have to apply for a visa outside of the country—here or in Jordan."

"That's easy enough; we'll just bring Ali and Narges here," I said. Problem solved!

The clerk held up his hand like a stop sign. "Which brings us to problem number two," he said. "The United States is being very careful about granting travel visas to Iraqis since 9/11. I'm sure you can understand the government's responsibility to protect the American people."

"Actually . . . ," I began, set to give this guy an earful about what I did understand after visiting two hospitals in Basra and seeing hundreds of innocent children and families whose lives had been blown apart by war. Didn't we also have a responsibility to help them? Asko firmly took my arm and I clamped my mouth shut, letting him take over until I cooled off.

"But they are granting some visas, right?" Asko asked. "How do we get one?"

"It's not that easy," the clerk said. "You have to send a written request to Homeland Security for humanitarian parole."

"But that could take months, and Ali needs help right now." So many other children's lives depended on me helping this one child to come to the United States for medical care he couldn't get in his own country. We didn't have time to spend faxing letters and leaving voicemails that wouldn't get returned. I'd gone that route in Bosnia and knew this was going to be even tougher.

During the next six months, I wrote dozens of emails to NGOs in Washington, Kuwait, and Baghdad, and to congressmen and senators in New York and New Jersey, inquiring if someone could help me to get visas for Ali and Narges. Looking back, I can see that I was obsessed. It wasn't good for my health or my marriage, but I couldn't let it go. So much was at stake, not just for Ali but for all of the children who were suffering in hospitals like the one I'd found him in. So often, people say they want to help. But few actually do anything. I knew that I actually could help, if only I could get Ali here. That made all of the roadblocks that much more maddening, emailing one place and getting directed somewhere else, sometimes a month later being directed back to the original person I had contacted.

Meanwhile, to complicate matters, I had lost track of Ali and Narges. He had checked out of the hospital in mid-June, shortly after I left Kuwait, and there was no record of where he and his family lived—or if their home was even still standing. Dr. Ahmed couldn't find them; Mohammed with the HOC couldn't

Mommy and Daddy,
in his Merchant Marine uniform

Frankie and me sitting on the
stoop of 71 Major Avenue

Alfie and me
at the Jersey Shore

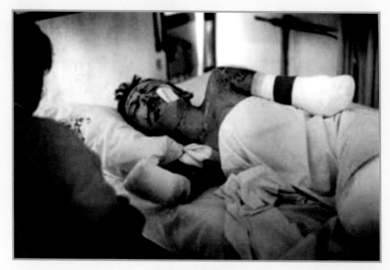

Kenan in the hospital in Maglaj, after the blast that forever changed his life

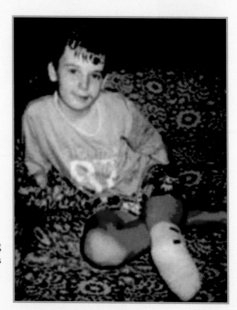

Kenan in Toronto preparing
for his prosthesis

Kenan walks me down the aisle to Asko.

Walking through the halls of an Iraqi hospital

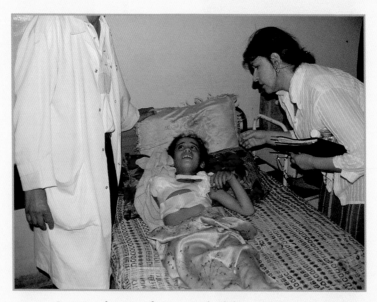

Learning the story of an Iraqi girl, while touring hospitals

Asko and Ali, showing off
his new arm

Ali and Lauren at the beach,
the closest of friends

Ahmed smiling,
after he received his new eyes

Christina and me at Iraqi border with Ahmed, Ali, and family

Kenan, Dr. Kaveh Alizadeh, and me at a fundraiser for GMRF

Fabian, Sarah, and me outside their collapsed home in Haiti

Posing with my Haitian girls in Staten Island

*Left to right*: Sajjad, Sajjad, Fareeda, Hussein, and Abdeen

*Clockwise from left*: Ermina, Jasmin, me, Sajjad, Sajjad,
Malak, Abdeen, and Fareeda

find them. I was receiving occasional emails from Narges, short notes using a few words that said so much: *When Ali come? Why no write?* I was frantic to get word to them, but my emails always bounced back. I couldn't assure them that they were very much in my thoughts, that I was still trying to keep my promise however I could.

Several months went by with no word at all from Narges, when one night I opened my email to find this letter. I later learned that Narges had asked another teacher who knew some English to write.

*By The Name of God*
*Dear Elissa.*
*I'd like to go directly to my subject without any introductories.*

*It is very long when you promised the child (Ali) to treat him. He now began to live a new kind of life which is the kind of hopeless from his life. He lost the hope of your help to him and that is because that long period.*

*Now, he is suspicious of that your help, and when I try to calm him down , he always says "They are foreign people. They can do whatever they say, but because they don't do anything up to now that means they don't want to help me"*

*Dear Elissa*
*I—as the child unte—ask you by the right of God to do one of two things. Either to present your real help or to tell him that you can not help him.*

*I'm very sure that it is very very difficult for him when you say that you can not help him, but I'm also sure that it is more*

*easy for him than to live in a dream of your help. It is more easy*
*for him than his waking up from his dream and finds himself*
*losing his hand and his hope.*

*I ask you by the right of Jesus Christ who sacrifices his life*
*for the sake of the weak. I ask you by the right of each child—*
*(whether they are Iraqi or foreign children)—who has lost his*
*right to live his life peacefully without any obstacles.*

*PLEASE ANSWER ME AS FAST AS YOU CAN.*

*WITH MY BEST*

*WISHES, Narges*

I sat at my desk, reading this note twice, then again. I imagined Narges trying to comfort her nephew, telling him not to
give up but also not wanting to give him false hope. *I'm here and
I'm still trying. I won't give up.* I wrote the words, praying this
time they would make it through. I held my breath as I hit the
send button. "C'mon, please," I coaxed, staring at the screen,
but the email rebounded immediately. "Ali, I'm not going to
forget about you," I said, hitting the resend button twice even
though I knew it was futile.

"Babe, this isn't healthy. You need to sleep," Asko called from
our bed.

"How can I sleep? Narges is emailing me, I can't get ahold of
them or make any progress."

"There's nothing more you can do," Asko said, and rolled
over. "Do us both a favor and accept that for just six or seven
hours at night."

I couldn't blame Asko for being short with me. I'd leave the
computer on when I went to sleep, and every time I heard a *ding*

I'd jump out of bed. This had been going on for months. I'd be up either checking emails or pacing the bedroom, worrying and waiting. The truth was that the charity had become a twenty-four/seven endeavor, and it was wearing on me, Asko, and our marriage—but I also knew that this wasn't going to change anytime soon.

I went to bed, lying awake with my mind racing. I was as still as possible so as not to wake up Asko. That's when I had the idea to break into my walk-in closet across the hall, next to the bathroom, and turn it into an office. I could slide my desk into the corner, and there was just enough room to fit some shelves along the back wall. "Babe, do you think you could put a window in that closet, so I can see the ocean over the tree-tops?" I asked.

"Yeah, sure," Asko mumbled. "Anything. Just go to sleep."

It felt good to at least solve one problem. My office has been in that closet ever since, even when we started renting office space for volunteers down the street from my house. It still kills me to think any of my kids are trying to reach me and need me, and maybe think I've forgotten about them. Today I sleep with a BlackBerry next to my bed, and I still snap awake when I hear the *ding* of an email or text coming in.

———

Lots of people call and email me, offering advice and telling me what to do, so Christina Frank's phone call was refreshing. This woman was just honest: She wanted to help. She didn't know how. "What can I do?" she kept asking. Christina reminded me of me, sitting in Mo's office. I liked her immediately and knew we would wind up being close friends.

Christina seemed surprised when I answered the GMRF phone line at nine o'clock on a Tuesday night, but for me nine o'clock was part of my work day. And besides, my home number and the charity number were one and the same back then. The forty-two-year-old mom from Virginia had read a story about me in *Parade* magazine that mentioned my trip to Iraq. "Actually, it was my seven-year-old daughter's idea for me to call you," she said. "Lauren was complaining about being bored with nothing to do, just a few days after Christmas, mind you. I launched into one of those speeches every mom gives their kids now and then about how lucky she is to have so much. I read her Ali's story, about everything he'd gone through and the trouble you're having to bring him here for a new hand. Lauren looked straight at me and said, 'So, let's call this woman and ask if we can help to bring Ali here.' Believe me, calling a stranger I read about in a magazine isn't something I'd ever done before. But how could I say no to my daughter?"

*How could I say no?* How many times had I said these exact words myself. I told Christina the trouble I was having trying to get Homeland Security to grant humanitarian parole for Ali and Narges. Wouldn't you know it? Christina was the director of criminal justice services for a suburb of Washington, D.C., and knew just how to work through the government's bureaucracy. We were both excited about the thought of teaming up to help Ali. "I'm doing this for me as much as for Lauren." She told me how, for twelve years, she had worked supervising two thousand criminals on probation—some who were trying to get their lives back on track and others who really weren't trying at all. She had been feeling more and more burnt-out in recent years. She needed something to spark her passion again, to make her feel like she was doing something right for the world.

"I know exactly what you mean." I wound up telling Christina about how Kenan had been the catalyst for me starting GMRF and totally recharging my own life. I even told her about my panic attacks after losing the people I loved most; that's how comfortable I felt with her. And she told me about her own deeply personal recent loss. A dear friend had been battling with lung cancer for years, and she'd been in remission for a long time. But just a few months ago, Jane had called Christina to tell her that the cancer was back and spreading fast. Her doctor predicted she'd have only a few healthy months left.

"The diagnosis was horrible, but Jane also saw it as an opportunity to finally do the things she'd been putting off for years," Christina told me as I poured another cup of tea. I felt as if she were right in the kitchen with me, sitting across the table.

"What did she do?" I asked. Even though I hadn't been close to death, I knew what it was like to hit rock bottom and then decide to live the life you really want to live.

"She quit her job, bought a mobile home, and traveled around the country, checking off items on her bucket list, as long as she could. I'm someone who has always played it safe, followed the rules, and when Jane died last month it really hit me hard. I started asking myself questions and questioning my life. What kind of footprint will I have left on the world? And how can I be a better role model to my children? Funny, it turned out that my daughter was a role model for me."

During that hour-long phone call, we laughed and we cried

together. I've never become so close with someone so fast. Christina had dialed the phone thinking to donate some money, but by the time we hung up we'd made a lunch date for a few weeks later. Even though I had no idea what Christina looked like, I knew the pretty blonde woman with sparkling blue eyes and a warm smile coming toward me at the train station was her. We hugged, and it was like reconnecting with an old friend.

"I feel like I'm in a sitcom episode," Christina said, both of us laughing while the GMRF Bosnian fraternity—Kenan, Boro, and Asko—cracked jokes in English and Bosnian. We were driving around the windy streets of the West Village, Asko behind the wheel and Boro giving him directions to a trendy bistro he wanted to take us to.

While we ate, Christina laid out a plan she and Lauren had come up with. Lauren had talked to her second grade class at Jennie Dean Elementary School and her Brownie troop about writing letters to Virginia congressman Frank Wolf, explaining Ali's case and how they wanted to bring the boy here to help him and learn more about Iraq. Christina would hand deliver the letters to Wolf's assistant, who thought the kids might actually have some clout in convincing the congressman to take up the boy's case. Wolf had been to Iraq several times and was known for his involvement in humanitarian causes worldwide. Boro was so impressed that he offered to pay for Christina and me to go to Kuwait to pick up Ali and Narges if Congressman Wolf came through with humanitarian parole. "I'd be honored to go with Elissa, but I'll pay my own way," Christina insisted, which impressed all of us even more. By the end of that lunch, we all knew we had a new partner and we were all excited to put our plan into action.

————

Christina's family and entire community were as excited as she and I were to become involved in Operation Ali. Lauren's class got busy spreading the word to their parents, and within just a few weeks members of the community had dropped off five big suitcases with toys and school supplies for Ali and the kids at the hospitals I had visited in Basra. People at Christina's office and her husband's office, and their neighbors and friends, chipped in too. Christina and I spoke or emailed every other day; she was so proud of her daughter and their community. "I feel like my soul is coming back to life," she told me. "I've volunteered before, but there's something special about bringing all of these people together to help one child."

"It's more personal," I said. "And when Ali comes here and gets his new hand, you'll really see what a difference you and Lauren have made in this kid's life."

But we did wait—and wait—and that was the hard part. Christina called Congressman Wolf's office in early February 2004 and made an appointment to see his aide, Judy McCary. Christina went armed with a letter from Ali's doctor in Iraq saying he needed a prosthetic hand, a letter from Shriners approving treatment, birth certificates for Ali and Narges, a letter from the Kuwait Ministry of Interior inviting me to stay in Kuwait, and nearly a hundred letters that Lauren and her friends had written. McCary was duly impressed. But two weeks later, she called Christina with discouraging news: even though Congressman Wolf was touched by the outpouring of support for Ali from his constituents, he couldn't find any shortcuts for bringing them here. The good news was that he was willing to write a letter to Homeland Security urging them to grant Ali humanitarian parole. Christina then began filling out the pile of paperwork for the humanitarian parole application, and I worked to supply all of the documentation—another letter from Ali's doctor saying he needed to travel for medical purposes, a letter from me promising I would support Ali and Narges while they were here, birth certificates—and a cover letter from Congressman Wolf.

Finally, in early February, things began to go our way. First, Mohammed hooked me up with Dr. Luma Sabah al-Beaty, a physician at Talemi Hospital in Iraq who worked for an organization called IOM that referred children to the HOC. She said her organization would help us find Ali, and personally drove around Basra for a week with a photo that Mohammed had given her of the boy. It turned out that Ali and his aunt's family were living just three blocks from the hospital! I was so relieved to have found them, even though I still couldn't give them the good news they wanted to hear.

Three weeks later, my phone rang. It was Christina.

"Elissa, you'd better sit down," she said.

"Christina, don't even say that to me. What?"

"No really, sit down," she said, and I couldn't tell by her voice if it was good news.

"Okay, I'm sitting." I was perched on the edge of my chair, my heart pounding wildly.

"We got it," she said, and I heard Lauren and her little brother, Alex, cheering in the background. Then, Christina and

I both started screaming and laughing. I danced around the room, and I knew she was doing the same with her kids. "We did it, Mom! We did it!" I heard these little voices yell with excitement.

"Give your kids a high five from me," I said. Meanwhile, I was already typing an email for Dr. Luma to deliver to Narges: *Thank you for not giving up on me. Our prayers have been answered. I'm coming soon to get you and Ali.*

———

"C'mon, where are they?" I said, taking off my sunglasses and squinting against the blue-brown desert sky as if I might actually see better. There was sand in my eyes, my nose, my mouth. When I wiped my forehead with my shirt sleeve, it felt like I was actually rubbing even more grit on my face.

"They'll be here, Elissa. Soon—I'm sure of it," Christina said, but she too stood on tiptoes, following my gaze, her lips pursed. Her shoulder-length blonde hair was tied up under a scarf, her blue eyes hidden behind big, round Jackie O sunglasses. I could pass for Arab with my dark hair and olive complexion, but Christina's alabaster skin and sun-blushed cheeks were a dead giveaway that she was a stranger here. Even in Kuwait, she had been stared at since the moment we had stepped off the plane the previous morning. We spent the day at the Kuwait Ministry of Health getting some final papers for Ali, and then at the HOC office, firming up the details of getting Ali and Narges safely out of Iraq. I had wanted to meet them at the hospital in Basra, but Mohammed said it wasn't safe for us to travel back there again. The fighting was more heated than when I'd been there a year earlier. So, instead, we arranged to bring Ali and Narges to the border, in a hospital ambulance instead of an official-looking jeep, for added protection.

Christina and I were both exhausted. We'd been waiting at the border station for more than three hours, since around the time the sun came up over the desert. During our first night in Kuwait we had snagged only a few hours of sleep. Around eleven o'clock, after a long day of running around, people started showing up at our hotel room. Mohammed, who was our first guest, told us that Kuwaitis take a nap for a few hours in the dead heat of the afternoon, do business in the evening, and eat dinner around midnight. By one in the morning, we'd had four or five visitors, bringing food and wishing us luck. We were eating yet another snack with Nafisah and her husband when there was a sharp rap on the door.

"Miss, you'll have to leave this door open," the hotel manager informed us in a crisp Arabic accent. "Or, better yet, meet with your male guests in the lobby." Christina and I exchanged a puzzled look, and Nafisah had her hand to her mouth, suppressing a smile, as the manager gave us and our room a long, suspicious once-over, his arms crossed in disapproval. After he left, Nafisah cleared up our confusion. "It seems that he believed you might be running a brothel," she explained, and we all fell apart, laughing.

Now, I saw Christina checking her wristwatch again and I gently elbowed her, trying to break the tension.

Christina smiled weakly. "Don't look, but that guard keeps staring at us," she whispered. There were four Iraqi soldiers in green fatigues with guns tucked into their belts patrolling the small area where we were. Security had definitely gotten tighter since Asko and I had traveled to Basra a year ago. This time we had been asked to get out of the jeep and were heavily questioned at the Kuwait border, the guard reading and rereading the documents from the Kuwait Ministry of Health, the Shriners Children's Hospital where Ali was to be treated, and Homeland Security. He kept asking Mohammed why two American women would be transporting Iraqis across the border. Mohammed was looking a little worried after about twenty minutes. Finally the guard made a phone call, probably to a superior to ask what he should do. We all breathed a sigh of relief when he opened the gate and let us through.

The one-room cement building where Christina and I were instructed to wait for Ali had just a tiny window and a fan blowing hot air. It wasn't any better than standing outside in the hot sun, staring at the highway that seemed to lead into the sand. The only relief was a few luxurious minutes here and there of blasting the AC in the jeep.

After a few more hours, I couldn't stand being in that stuffy room or outside in the hot sun any longer. I tried calling Dr. Luma, who was escorting the ambulance from the hospital. "Still no reception. C, I'm getting really nervous. What if . . ."

My voice trailed off and I just looked at Christina, thinking about all that still had to happen before we were set to board a plane back to New York in two days. When and if Ali and Narges did show up at the border, we still had to go to the American embassy for their visas to get into the United States and then to the British embassy to get transfer visas for the overnight stay in London. Neither of these important documents was a done deal, even with humanitarian parole. In short: a lot could still go wrong.

"Hey, we got this far," Christina said, although her smile was tight and her voice sounded as shaky as I felt. I pulled myself together and smiled back. That's how it's always been with Christina and me, and it still is. We have this great give-and-take: when one of us is losing it, the other one steps up to put on a positive face. And even if we're both in trouble, someone will at least be able to crack a joke.

"Okay, what's so funny?" Christina asked, her features relaxing as I started laughing softly.

"I was just thinking of last night, our wild brothel. We'd better not quit our day jobs, right?"

We fell into each others' arms, laughing for a few moments, then Christina took off her sunglasses and wiped the tears from her eyes. "Can you believe this, E? We're really here. After six months of sawing through reams of red tape, a year after you met this kid, we're really here. He's got to show up; he's just got to."

———

We saw the ambulance in the distance—or at least we thought we did. A boxy green vehicle that could have been an ambulance or an army jeep, the details blurry in the midday sun, was approaching the security gate on the Iraq side of the border. Then, it just disappeared. "Relax, they're just asking them some questions," Mohammed said after ten minutes. Then, it was fifteen minutes, thirty minutes.

"You did see something, right?" I asked Christina. She nodded and grabbed my hand. We both hung on tightly to each other, barely daring to breathe. What if the border guards turned them back? Finally we saw a black sedan moving slowly from the security station toward us. The back window was rolled down and Ali stuck his head out. "Elissa, Elissa!" he yelled, waving.

Christina and I hugged each other, and then we both started crying, a floodgate of emotions busting loose. I ran to the car and Ali jumped out, still shouting my name. He looked so handsome in dark dress pants and a matching button-down shirt, shiny loafers on his feet. I later learned that Ali's family is quite poor and his relatives all chipped in to buy new outfits for both him and Narges to wear to America. They had one small bag between them.

"I told you I'd come back," I said. He grinned even wider, nodding as if he understood.

Narges greeted me and Christina both with a huge hug. "Thank you, Elissa," she said, her voice shaky. "Please forgive, my English bad."

"No, very good," I encouraged. "Very good."

"The boy doesn't lose faith," she said. "All this time, he knows you come. He believes. Bless you, and bless Doctor Luma."

"Where is she?" I asked, and Narges pointed to the security building near the gate they'd passed through.

"They didn't let her through the checkpoint because she doesn't have a visa to get into Kuwait," said Mohammed, who was on his cell phone.

"I wanted to thank her," I said, a jolt of disappointment deflating the moment. Luma was the shepherd who had brought

Ali to me. We'd become so close, emailing back and forth for the past four months while she was looking for Ali and Narges. We had both been so excited to finally meet, and now she was so close that I could have run to her. Mohammed handed me his phone. "Luma, is that you?" I asked.

"Elissa, I love you," she said.

"I love you too," I said, looking at this beautiful boy who was grabbing my hand with his, and hiding his other wounded arm behind his back. This woman I had never met, and I might never meet, had gone through an incredible experience with me. Luma and I teamed up, across the globe, to keep a promise to a child. We shared a special bond: love, pure and simple. When it comes down to it, that's really why I do what I do— and it's why so many people have helped me and continue to help me. Love.

## CHAPTER FOURTEEN

# Ali's Dream

❧

"This is all a dream, yes?" Narges whispered, so as not to awaken her nephew on his first night in the room that would be his for the next two months. We sat—she on the end of Ali's bed, me on the colorful ABC rug on the floor—watching Ali sleep, hugging a huge brown teddy bear with a red bow that Lauren had given to him, one foot kicked out from under the blanket.

"A dream come true, for us all," I said, pulling the blanket gently over Ali's foot, smiling as I recalled the look of pleased disbelief on the boy's face when I told him this bedroom was all his. At home, in the small house he shared with Narges and his grandmother, he was used to sleeping on a mat on the cement floor of the main room. And this was a beautiful room! Home Depot and Ikea had donated $30,000 worth of materials and furniture to transform the former drab room at Mount Loretto. Now, there were three bedrooms, a bathroom, a living space, and a beautiful kitchen there for my kids. Dozens of workers from the Home Depot and Ikea stores in New Jersey and New York had donated their time to have a weekend remodeling party.

I knew exactly what Narges meant about this feeling unreal; it was hard to believe we were all finally here after two long days of travel. Despite the drama of trying to get Ali out of Iraq, our time in Kuwait City was so joyful. Christina and I had both wanted to spoil Ali and give this boy, who had spent the last year ashamed to leave his house, a chance to play and be a kid again. His eyes lit up in delight as he pushed the buttons on the hotel elevator, watching with amazement as the doors opened at each floor. Ali rode the elevator up and down, again and again. The hotel was Moroccan-style, with carved wooden balconies on each floor, dripping with lush greenery, and brass wall accents and pillars that Ali thought were gold. The high ceilings reverberated the noise of Ali running back and forth on each floor, calling and waving to us as we stood in the lobby. I didn't have the heart to stifle all of this wonderful energy, even after the manager complained, so we headed to the big colorful downtown marketplace, Souk al-Mubarakiya, the oldest market in the city.

We wandered in and out of the shops, which sold everything from vintage Middle Eastern hookahs and brass lamps, to high-end gold jewelry, to fresh fruit and bakery goods. Christina bought Narges and Ali a few changes of clothes, and I looked for souvenirs for Kenan and Asko. Ali kept grabbing my hand, pulling me among the maze of stalls set up in the square. He ran his hand over stacks of jewel-toned Persian rugs that, to him, could easily have been magic carpets. Men in turbans stood at wooden tables, puzzling over backgammon and drinking thick coffee, surrounded by big burlap bags overflowing with heaps of gold and brown grains, red and black beans.

Women in head scarves and long Western skirts or traditional Muslim cloaks stood at tables laid out with bakery goods in all shapes and sizes—from the Middle Eastern flat bread eaten with every meal to European croissants and gooey pastries that oozed jam or chocolate. Ali kept looking up at me, squeezing my hand, saying, "I love you, Elissa. I love you." It was all the English he knew, but the words seemed to convey everything he needed to say.

At one point, Narges just stopped to gaze around the bustling square, wiping tears from her eyes. I touched her arm and she gave me the saddest smile. "Basra, before war," she said, sweeping her hand to take in the thriving carnival of colors and activities surrounding us. "Now . . ." She dropped her hand heavily to her side and shook her head. I hugged her; there were no words. It was hard to believe that her homeland, now riddled with bombed-out buildings and markets where a child could pick up a land mine and lose his hand or worse, had once been as pristine and prosperous as Kuwait City.

After Ali fell asleep in the hotel room that night, while Nafisah and her husband were over to share a midnight meal with us, Narges told us more about her nephew's life. "There was no room in the house of Ali's parents, who had six other children," Nafisah said, translating for Narges. "Ali was the oldest—now almost a man at age thirteen—so he went to live with his father's sister and mother several years ago. His father relied on him to be the man of that household, and he took that responsibility very seriously."

"Almost a man," I said, shaking my head, glancing over at the big brown stuffed bear that Christina's daughter had sent with us for Ali. We'd given him the bear when we picked him up at the border, and he'd carried it around all day. Christina had showed him photos of Lauren—a petite girl with long golden hair and blue-gray eyes like her mother, and a smile to rival Ali's—as well as her five-year-old son, Alex. She told Ali how seven-year-old Lauren had convinced her as well as her friends and classmates to help him come to America. Lauren was Ali's hero; he couldn't wait to meet her.

"You must understand, it's not unusual to be married at age seventeen for boys, fourteen or fifteen for girls," Nafisah said. "The young men must learn to care for the women, and this is what Ali's father was trying to teach his son. Part of this lesson was helping his father to sell gasoline at the market and earn money. His father depended on him to do this, but it is not possible without a hand. Ali feels terribly guilty about letting his family down. And his father is still very angry about what happened. Sometimes, the boy feels that anger is toward him instead of the situation."

I crept into the room where Ali slept and placed the teddy bear next to him, just in case he woke up and was afraid. I thought of the many dreams that would come true for this boy over the next eight weeks.

————

Ali was more excited to visit the suburban Virginia town where Christina and her family lived than he was to go into Manhattan. There was something—or rather someone—he wanted to see even more than the Statue of Liberty or the Empire State Building: the little girl who had given him the teddy bear he was hanging on to throughout our five-hour road trip the day after he arrived in Staten Island. We had a few days until his first doctor appointment, and besides, I already missed Christina. During our trip to Kuwait, we had become even closer. She was Thelma to my Louise, and that trip was the first of three we'd make to Kuwait to pick up more Iraqi kids during the next few years while Asko stayed in Staten Island working and taking care of whatever needed to be done with the charity.

My van was packed to the gills with luggage, food, and gifts for Lauren and Alex, whom I'd never met. Ali and Nafisah's two young children who were traveling with her sat in the far back. Nafisah sat with Narges and me in the middle, and Kenan was riding shotgun next to Rita Lu's son Louis, on summer break from film school, who was driving. It was a long drive, but it seemed to fly by compared to the fourteen hours of travel from Kuwait we'd endured just two days earlier. The kids taught the adults in the front seats some of their favorite Arabic children's songs, including one that was a driving song. The chorus was something about driving me to get married.

When we arrived in Manassas, Narges and Nafisah jumped out of my van to hug Christina and meet her children, who were waiting for us on their front lawn. I was surprised that Ali hung back a bit, clinging to my side, hiding his arm behind his back. This was the first time that I realized how shy he is, and how much courage it took for him to wave me over in the hospital the first time we met. Lauren was shy too, smiling at Ali, then giving her mother a wide-eyed *What should I say?* look. Alex, being five, asked Ali if he wanted to see his new red wagon parked in the driveway.

"Hey, can I try out your new wheels?" Kenan asked, pretending to hop onto a tiny wagon. Everyone laughed, breaking the tension.

"We've got a bicycle built for two," Lauren piped up, running into the garage to get the other bike. That got Ali's attention; his face lit up and he said something excitedly to Narges.

"He very much wants bike in Iraq, but no money," Narges said, then she turned to Nafisah to say more in Arabic.

"He wants to ride, but he doesn't know how," Nafisah said.

"I'll teach you," Lauren said, getting onto the front seat. "C'mon, Ali."

Narges tried coaxing Ali onto the back seat but he shook his head and looked at the ground.

"I'll go first," Kenan said. He went into the van to take off his prosthetic arms so that he could grip the handlebars with his elbows. Ali and Alex ran after the bike as Lauren and Kenan cruised around the block, then it was Ali's turn. He sat gingerly on the backseat and Kenan took the front seat. Narges stood to one side of Ali and Kenan to the other, partially to help him balance, but mostly for moral support. We all cheered and clapped as the bike took off slowly down the driveway. Then Christina grabbed my arm and waved toward her neighbor's house across the street.

"Don't look now, but we're making a bit of a spectacle," she said. The neighbors all around were looking through their windows, coming out on their porches to watch the circus that had come to town. Suddenly, I saw this scene through a stranger's eyes: Kenan with no arms and Nafisah in full *hijab* running down the street beside this bicycle with one-armed Ali and Lauren laughing and shrieking. Alex was in close pursuit pull-

ing his red wagon, followed by Nafisah's kids. And my nephew
Louis—who resembles a young, better-looking Jerry Garcia
with long hair and sixties-style glasses—was running along,
filming the whole thing.

"Never a dull moment, right?" I said, as the bicycle brigade
pulled up in front of us and all of the kids toppled into a pile on
the lawn, laughing.

After that, the ice was cracked wide open for Ali and Lauren.
They spent the rest of the afternoon in the basement rec room
playing foosball and air hockey. Ali roughhoused with Alex
and Nafisah's kids, letting them pin him down and pretending
to be trapped, then breaking free and running away. All the
while Lauren and Ali had an ongoing charades game of transla-
tion. She pointed to parts of her face, "eyes, nose, mouth . . . ,"
and then he held up his good hand, pointing to his features and
telling her the Arabic words, which she repeated with some
success. Within a few hours, it was like the two of them were
old friends, Lauren talking to Ali in English and him answering
in Arabic. And somehow, they seemed to really understand
each other. I've seen this time and again, with kids from Haiti
and Iraq, Libya and Africa. Kids can communicate no matter
where they come from. They all seem to have a universal language. They don't have the fears of adults. They aren't closed
off. They just find something to laugh about together, and that's
that.

"Follow me," Lauren said, grabbing Ali's hand to take him
upstairs to her bedroom. She took a shoebox out from under
her bed, filled with copies of dozens of letters written by her
classmates and Brownie troop members to Congressman Wolf.

Ali picked up the letters, all neatly written in cursive on lined white paper, and looked at them while Nafisah read parts in English, then Arabic. Many letters read something like this: *Please give Ali permission to come here so he can have a new arm and a better life. We also want to learn more about his country, and what it's like to be a kid in a country that's so different. What's it like to go to school, play, and grow up when there's a war going on? He did nothing wrong, and deserves our help.* I listened, my chest welling up.

A blush spread across Ali's cheeks, along with an ear-to-ear grin, while Nafisah was reading. "All of these children who don't know me wrote letters to help me?" he said softly when she was finished. He looked at Lauren. "Thank you, I love you," he said, and she gave him a big hug.

Christina, Narges, and I were watching from the doorway.

"Beautiful," I whispered to Narges, who then began crying harder.

"Forgive me," she said, wiping her cheeks.

There was nothing to forgive.

Lauren had taken out a photo album and was showing Ali family photos, so we left them alone and went downstairs. Christina made tea, and Narges spoke in Arabic for a few minutes, then Nafisah told us why Ali's aunt was crying. "Ali changed after the accident. She says, as time passed, he began to doubt you would come back to help him. His sadness was turning to anger."

"I never forgot you and Ali," I said, taking both of Narges's hands.

"Many young men with injuries this bad become beggars on

the street or turn to violence, and Ali's aunt and his mother worried about his future," Nafisah continued.

"But Ali is here now, he's happy," I said to Narges. "Ali is okay."

Narges nodded, speaking quickly. "That's why she cries," Nafisah translated. "She is filled with relief to see Ali so happy. To see him meeting the American girl who cared enough to help him. And then the letters from so many children . . . all of this love is healing for the boy. Yes, the hospital will heal his hand. But these children heal Ali's heart."

Now I was crying even harder than Narges. I realized that this little charity I had started six years ago had the potential to give children so much more than new limbs. We were building bridges of compassion and understanding between kids who lived across the globe. I looked over at Christina, who was also wiping at her eyes. "I know," she said. "This is big, E. Really big."

The next day when we visited Lauren's school, I saw the potential of GMRF to build bridges between cultures play out tenfold. The electronic billboard in front of the building had big blinking lights that shouted JENNIE DEAN STUDENTS WELCOME ALI!!!! Ali and Lauren were both thrilled to see this. He was nervous, hanging on to Lauren's hand, as they stood on the front lawn and the students came outside to meet him. "Just be yourself," Lauren whispered, giving Ali a thumbs-up. "They like you—friends!"

Lauren's teacher introduced Ali to each of her thirty students, and he greeted each one of them with a hug and a kiss. Then, they took him into their classroom for an exchange of questions. Lauren's classmates didn't ask about the war or even how Ali had lost his hand, but they were more interested in typical kid stuff: What's your favorite American food? *Potato chips*. How is it different in Iraq than here? *It's so colorful here; in Iraq it's mostly gray from the desert dirt*.

"What does your school look like and how often do you go?" the kids wanted to know. At that point the schools in Iraq were closed because of the fighting. Ali said he wanted to go back to school, he missed learning and being with his friends. But the American kids thought he was the luckiest guy in the world, not having to sit through math and science lessons. As for Ali, he couldn't believe that all of these kids received a hot lunch every day in the cafeteria. The kids groaned, telling him that he wasn't missing much. But I knew that it wasn't unusual for Ali to miss lunch altogether. When we left after a few hours, some of the students asked Ali to be their pen pal, and they gave him their addresses. As for Ali's address, there are no street names and numbers except in the business districts. Instead, his address was something like: three blocks from the post office, across from the big cypress tree.

"Fun?" I asked in the car on the way home.

"Fun," Ali said, putting his fist to his heart. "Friends."

———

Ali fidgeted, excited and nervous that the day when he was to receive his new hand had finally arrived. He hummed "Heart and Soul," the piano duet that Christina had taught him to play with her daughter, and kept taking a small photo of Lauren out of his pocket. They had exchanged photos on our last night in

Virginia, and Lauren had slept with Ali's photo under her pillow for the past two months. Ali kept her photo in his pocket, patting it occasionally as if to secure it in its place close to his heart. Lauren and Christina were coming to visit later today. It was a bittersweet occasion: the celebration of Ali's new hand and a time to say good-bye before he and Narges went back to Iraq in a few weeks.

Ali adjusted the white baseball cap with the Shriners logo that a nurse had just given him, running his hand along the brim that shaded his eyes. Kenan sat across from him in the hospital waiting room. "It's much cooler with the brim to the back," he said, reaching out to reposition the cap. Ali smiled, playfully batting away Kenan's hand, saying something in Arabic.

"Like this." Kenan slowly turned the brim of an imaginary hat on his own head.

"Ahhh," Ali said, giving him a thumbs-up, then pulling the brim down over the back of his head. "This?"

Kenan gave Ali a high five with his prosthetic hand, as easily as if it were skin and bones, and Ali hugged him. The two of them had become close over the past two months, Kenan protective like a big brother. He knew exactly what Ali was going through: the hospital visits, the media attention, the exciting and strange bustle of New York City. Kenan had insisted on coming along to all of Ali's appointments at Shriners Children's Hospital, two hours away in Philadelphia, even though he was busy with summer school and his part-time job working for GMRF. "He's going to need someone who knows what this is like, who can show him what the new hand can really do," he said.

And that's exactly what Kenan had done since day one, showing Ali how he could do everything from write, to open doors, to catch a soccer ball with his prosthetic hands. Kenan never actually explained to Ali how to do things; he just did them, and Ali watched and learned, becoming more confident as he watched Kenan.

Ali had first been to this hospital a week after arriving in Staten Island for his initial assessment with Dr. Scott Kozin, a renowned hand and upper extremities surgeon. Dr. Kozin, who has worked with many GMRF kids over the years, was pleased to see that Ali didn't need surgery. The amputation was clean, and the scars had healed over nicely. A week later we returned for the next big step: the fitting with the plastic mold that would provide a skeleton for Ali's new lower arm and hand. Kenan sat next to Ali, smiling reassuringly as the cast was placed over the boy's arm. Ali grimaced as he rubbed where the plastic met his skin. "It gets better," Kenan said, rubbing his own arm.

The doctor gave Ali a robotic hand and half arm to examine, explaining that he would also have an arm like this one that he could use to pick up and grasp things, as well as a non-mechanical sturdy cosmetic arm he could wear to play. Ali turned the hand and half arm over and over. He didn't really understand what the doctor was saying about how the cables were activated by muscle movement, even though Nafisah was there to translate. Kenan rolled up his sleeve, pointing to the cables on his own arm and showing Ali how he could move his shoulder a certain way to open his fingers, another way to close them. Ali watched Kenan do this several times, his features relaxing. Kenan picked up a pencil. "See?" he said. Ali nodded, a mischievous smile spreading across his face as he held up his arm cast like a sword, pretending to challenge Kenan to a duel.

Now, Kenan kept glancing warily at the four or five reporters who had come with cameramen and microphones to cover Ali's big day. They were interviewing me and Narges on the opposite side of the waiting room; I'd made it clear that Ali wasn't available until after his appointment. I'd learned a thing or two since Kenan's first visit. I still couldn't stand up for myself very well, but I could stand up for my kids. Still, one reporter snuck by me while I was busy talking to one of the doctors, answering some questions that had to do with Ali's appointment. Out of the corner of my eye I saw a woman in a red suit charging across the room, mic in hand. I started to sprint after her, then stopped: Kenan was standing between her and Ali, smiling sweetly and holding up his hand like a stop sign. "We're busy right now, maybe later," he said, then turned to talk to Ali, his back to the reporter. He'd learned a thing or two too, and I was proud of him. Kenan had really become my second-in-command since Asko was busy working two jobs, even though he was busy with school and had big plans for a career in computer science.

It didn't take long to get Ali's prosthetic hand and forearm adjusted and fit onto his natural arm, and afterward we headed back to Mount Loretto to meet Christina and Lauren. Ali was so excited to show off his new arm, but frustrated too. The robotic arm was heavy, and moving the right muscles to make the fingers on the hand open and close wasn't coming easy to Ali. "You have to get strong, work out," Kenan told him through Nafisah. "Don't worry, it gets easier with time."

Our guests hadn't yet arrived when we got to Mount Loretto, so Kenan spent some time with Ali practicing some of the things he would perfect in physical therapy over the next few weeks before he went home—opening doors and windows, holding a cup, typing on the computer. My nephew Louis was also there, and at one point he and Kenan were looking out the window, whispering shyly about their mutual admiration of an attractive young woman, a reporter who was talking to Narges not far away. Ali didn't know exactly what they were saying, but he definitely knew what they were talking about. He opened the window, whistled, and waved the leggy blonde over! I'd never seen Kenan's face quite that shade of red, and Ali had a very mischievous grin on his face.

Ali kept glancing out the window, and finally he saw what he'd been waiting for: Lauren was getting out of her mother's car. There was a big grassy field between the main building and the parking lot, and both Lauren and Ali ran toward each other, holding out their arms, almost as if in slow motion like in the movies. They held hands, swinging their arms back and forth as they walked, Ali leading her toward the backyard so he could show her the soccer moves he'd been practicing with Kenan. That afternoon and evening they were inseparable, and Lauren insisted that she and her mother spend the night in a room with twin beds at Mount Loretto instead of a hotel. Both Ali and Lauren cried when it was time to say a final farewell the next morning. Christina, Narges, Nafisah, and I looked on. "Young love," I said, smiling, and the others sighed in agreement. Ali would grow into a man long before Lauren, who was six years younger than him. But for now these two children shared a special bond that would last for years.

## CHAPTER FIFTEEN

# Connecting the Dots

*June 2006*

*Ding!* I reached out my arm to answer the phone, an automatic response to the sound of the BlackBerry I now kept at my bedside while I slept. My global family had grown to more than eighty children and their families from Bosnia, Iraq, El Salvador, Russia, Indonesia, China, Sierra Leone, Pakistan, and Nepal. It didn't make sense to miss a call during their daytime when I'd have to wait to call back the next night. Plus, it was sometimes hard for me to get through. Answering the calls as they came in became my "normal." I worked around the clock on a never-ending "to do" list: buying warm coats and boots for kids experiencing winter cold and snow for the first time, arranging doctor visits and field trips to the zoo and museums, making travel arrangements, and—always—fielding requests from soldiers, reporters, and doctors about more kids who needed help.

"Hello?" I croaked, peeling open one eyelid: the clock read two a.m. There was only static on the other end, and I wasn't surprised that the caller ID showed an Iraqi phone number. I sat up and waited, smiling. It had been less than two months since he'd come here for a follow-up visit, but I needed to hear that sweet voice on the other end of the line.

"Elissa, Ali. I love you, Elissa. I love you."

"I love you too, Ali," I said. "Stay safe, sweetheart."

Neither one of us wanted to hang up. We both kept saying good-bye—me in English, he in Arabic—until all I heard was static again. I'd given Ali a cell phone and a few hours of time so he could call me, Kenan, Christina, and Lauren. He never called for more than a few minutes—mostly because he didn't know much English, but also to save his precious minutes. Besides, he had said all he really needed to say. So had I.

I held the phone against my cheek, wanting to hang on to my connection with Ali, thinking of his beautiful face when Lauren had shown him the box full of letters that she and her friends had written on his behalf nearly three years ago, restoring his faith. I could use a little of that right about now.

Word had spread fast throughout Basra about how Ali had received the new hand he was so proud of—both through word of mouth as well as the media—and within days of his return to Iraq I was flooded with dozens of requests from the British military base there, the U.S. military base, NGOs, and families all over Iraq. Even big government agencies with budgets I could only dream of were emailing and calling with requests. I, working out of my walk-in closet, was afraid to answer the phone because it might be bill collectors.

I felt a deep responsibility to the Iraqis, which had nothing to do with politics and everything to do with matters of the heart. To this day, after meeting people from all over the world, I still find that there's something especially warm about the

Iraqis. I've brought about twenty Iraqi children here to date, and each one has been so loving—hugging and kissing even the reporters and doctors they meet, exuding a genuine love that is truly inspiring. And the parents, siblings, aunts, and uncles who come as their guardians—most not knowing a word of English, many never having traveled outside of their region before—are so gracious and grateful. You see it in their eyes, and you hear it in their words even when you don't share the language. That's why it was so difficult for me when my charity and my kids became the target of negativity in a 9/11 backlash.

———

I had gotten used to people asking, "Why are you helping kids from other countries when there are so many needy kids here?" Over and over I tried to explain that I also worked to help local kids, but those kids got to go home to their own bedrooms after a doctor appointment or an afternoon of physical therapy. Most of the foreign children I worked with weren't that fortunate.

What I still wasn't used to, though, was how this question changed when I started bringing over kids from Iraq: "Why are you helping kids who are going to grow up to be terrorists?" It had been nearly five years since the attack on the World Trade Center, but our country was still recovering—particularly New Yorkers. There was no answer for the anger and pain except time, and eventually my kids would become part of the healing process. But the months after Ali left were particularly difficult.

The trouble at Mount Loretto actually began the very first day that Ali arrived. It was so subtle that I really noticed it only in retrospect—and by then it was too late. We threw a big party to welcome Ali and to showcase the gorgeous makeover that Home Depot and Ikea had done on the gloomy old orphanage. The Shriners were there, in their tasseled red hats, along with Arab women in long dark cloaks and festive scarves on their heads. I was so proud watching my kids from Bosnia and Iraq running around, laughing and shouting in all their different languages.

GMRF shared the Mount Loretto building with a day-care center, and I knew that some of the moms who dropped off their kids weren't crazy about the fact that there were foreigners staying there, even before the Iraqis. On the day of the party for Ali, it was hard to ignore some cool stares as they hustled their kids away from mine and into their SUVs. As always, I waved and smiled as if nothing was wrong. I knew some of these parents were scared and uninformed, but I never thought they'd actually take action on their bigotry.

A few months later, Bill, the assistant director at Mount Loretto, asked me to come into his office. He looked uncomfortable, barely meeting my gaze.

"Go ahead, tell me," I said, smiling even though I was nervous. "Are you raising the rent?" I was joking, since I didn't have any money to pay rent back then. I'd never been able to pay Mount Loretto a cent. I'll always be grateful to them for giving my charity its first real home, despite how our relationship ended.

"I don't know what to say, Elissa. This is crazy, but . . ." Bill pushed a piece of paper across the desk that looked like a memo of some kind.

"The Department of Health?" I read the memo, which was

apparently in response to a complaint someone had filed in reference to GMRF. "I don't understand . . ."

"An investigator has to check out all complaints," Bill said. "It's unfounded. See? He checked the box that says there are no grounds for any fines or charges."

"Let me get this straight," I said, dropping the paper onto Bill's desk like the garbage that it was. "Does this mean that someone complained about my kids being a health hazard?"

"I'm sorry, Elissa. The mothers at the day care are upset. It's been going on a long time, and I've been trying to keep things cool."

I shook my head, looking at the piece of paper. How could it be possible that these women—mothers—were trying to shut down GMRF?

"There's not much we can do except try to keep your kids out of the backyard while the day-care kids are there," Bill said, tapping steepled fingers together, obviously embarrassed. "We don't want any trouble. You understand."

No, actually, I didn't understand.

I'd like to say this was an isolated incident involving just a few overprotective moms. But the truth is, the holiday season brought out both the best and worst in Staten Island that year. People donated clothes and toys to the GMRF kids from Iraq and Bosnia who were staying at Mount Loretto, and our local paper ran a front-page article about the charity right before Christmas. It was nice to be supported by our community, but there were also a handful of letters to the editor that read something like this:

*. . . With the onset of the holidays and all that is going on around the globe, I found the article "Mangled Limbs" totally inappropriate. I am so offended by it that I am thinking of calling to cancel my subscription to the paper. As a mother of a 21-year-old veteran of "Operation Enduring Freedom" and "Operation Iraq Freedom" I don't think our young servicemen and women need to open their newspapers this morning and view this over their breakfast while being home for the holidays.*

About this time I was also beginning to receive emails from soldiers and military doctors who knew what was going on in Iraq. They all thanked me for helping when so many NGOs were leaving Iraq and had given up on trying to negotiate their way through the complicated system that would have allowed them to help some children. These were the letters that were important to me. I kept thinking of them as I faced the backlash that came that year. The response was disappointing, but I know that many Americans had complicated feelings about the war in Iraq, especially during that time. I decided to hold my head high, keep doing what I was doing, and focus on the work at hand. That was far more important than a nasty letter to the editor.

Some of the soldiers who reached out to me became my partners in bringing children here. The first military helper I had in Iraq was Major Norma G. Sandow, who was serving on the U.S. Army base in Baghdad. She wrote about a little boy who, at the age of five, was caught in the crossfire between insurgents and Iraqi soldiers on his way home from school. He raised his arm to shield his face, and in the process was horribly wounded. Now, he needed a prosthetic arm, as well as surgery to heal his scarred face and eyes that were sewn shut with twine.

The photo that Major Sandow attached of seven-year-old Ahmed showed a little boy whose face was badly disfigured by gunshot wounds, with bandages over his blind and scarred eyes. His strong, bright spirit came shining through, however, in his smile. I loved this brave little boy immediately.

———

That night after Ali called, I did what I do whenever I can't sleep but I'm too exhausted to get out of bed and work: I took Mommy's pink rosary beads from the bedside drawer where I keep them, hung on to them tightly, and prayed. I didn't even realize I was whispering the words aloud, "Dear God, I've made so many promises and now I'm really afraid I won't be able to keep them. Please help me."

Asko rolled over and threw his arm over me. "Go to sleep, babe. There's always tomorrow—and tomorrow's mail."

The truth was, funding had become a real issue, and I was beyond worried. Christina had been sending out appeals to foundations like crazy but without any luck. The major grant givers weren't interested in a small charity helping a handful of children; they wanted to see numbers: big staffs helping big numbers of children. But that's not what I do, and it never will be.

"It's no use. I can't sleep," I said. "I keep seeing their faces."

Asko pulled me closer; he knew exactly who I was talking about. "You have to stop torturing yourself," he said, and I heard just the slightest hint of irritation in his voice. "You can't afford to bring any more kids over. Not for now."

I couldn't blame Asko for losing patience; we'd had this conversation so many times during the past year. He was so logical, pointing out the simple math of the situation: I was now committed to more than forty children who had been here at least once during the past eight years and needed yearly follow-up visits. Despite Christina's fund-raising efforts, GMRF was still operating in 2006 on an annual budget of about $250,000—not much more than five years earlier—and bringing just one child and a guardian here costs about $8,000 to $10,000 per visit. Math was never my strong suit, but it was easy to see that our budget just wasn't keeping up with the growing number of kids coming to me who needed help. I had to start prioritizing even more carefully, but there were some cases that were easy to move to the top of the list. Ahmed was one of those cases.

The blind boy with the beautiful smile first came to Staten Island with his older brother Saad, age twenty-four, in March 2005 to receive a new arm and prosthetic eyes. It broke my heart seeing this little boy sitting in a wheelchair, his head bent. For the first month, Ahmed wouldn't smile or even respond when anyone but his brother spoke to him. "He's so ashamed of how he looks, and the ways he knows that people look at him," Saad told me. I knew that the doctors here could do better for him, and for the first time, I broke my rule about limiting medical care to prosthetics. How could I not?

Saad and I took Ahmed to see Dr. Pamela Gallin, a pediatric ophthalmologist at Columbia University Medical Center/NewYork-Presbyterian. I was so excited when she told us, after examining Ahmed, that there was a slim possibility that his eyesight might be able to be repaired to some extent. Maybe there were nerves that could be reconnected; maybe an artificial retina could be implanted. All I heard was the hope in the doctor's voice, not the caution.

Dr. Gallin referred us to an army of eye specialists, specialists in the cornea, the optic nerves, and parts of the eye I'd never heard of before. More than twenty doctors in all agreed to see Ahmed for free. They all said the boy reminded them of their own child or grandchild. He had this sweet way about him, and he was starting to come out of his shell a bit because so many people were rallying to help him. I'll never forget holding Saad in my arms, both of us in tears, when Dr. Gallin explained that the hospital had exhausted every possibility that Ahmed would ever be able to see again. Sadly, his retinas were too far deteriorated to ever work again. But still, she wasn't giving up hope. "It's not your eyes that see, but your brain," she explained. "Ahmed has five years of seeing and stored memories. That information never goes away. It's just a question of how to turn the vision part of the brain back on. It's not possible now, but perhaps in Ahmed's lifetime it will be."

As long as that possibility exists, I'm not giving up hope.

———

Ahmed went back to Iraq significantly better off than when he'd arrived here, but I knew there was still more I could do for him. I began to make plans for him to return as soon as enough time had passed that he needed to be refitted for a new prosthetic arm. I was ecstatic when my cousin Mimi, a teacher, got Ahmed into a great elementary school on Staten Island that has a program where he could learn Braille in Arabic as well as English.

Ahmed and his father came to Staten Island in July 2006 and stayed at Mount Manresa, the Jesuit retreat near my house where GMRF moved after Mount Loretto asked us to leave to make room for a "local charity," for the 2006–2007 school year. I spent time with them nearly every day. Asko kept warning me not to get too attached, but I couldn't help but fall in love with this boy who was learning to become a child again. Ahmed taught himself to play the piano at Mount Manresa, and he used to play the church organ in the chapel. Sister Maureen taught him "Frère Jacques" and "Mary Had a Little Lamb." He was also getting more occupational therapy, learning to walk with a cane and negotiate his surroundings. It was wonderful, watching him blossom during that year, even saying a few lines in a school play to a round of thunderous applause.

Once Ahmed began coming out of his shell, it was clear that he was a real character. He would call me on the cell phone I'd given to him, sometimes two or three times a day, even when we had plans to meet after his school day. Sometimes he called just to giggle and say, "I love you, Elissa." Or he'd say something like, "Elissa, *chaw belisha*."

I would slowly repeat what he said, waiting for him to correct me at least once. Ahmed was trying to teach me some Arabic. Or so I thought.

"Okay, *chaw belisha* to you too." This was met with peals of laughter. "That's not a word! Ahmed, you got me again."

"Yes," he said, still laughing. "Got you. I love you, Elissa, so much."

Ali Ameer, who was here to be fitted for a new arm, along with his aunt Narges, was a big part of giving little Ahmed back his smile during that summer. I'll never forget how sweet and protective Ali was, walking next to Ahmed and guiding him around the garden at Mount Manresa, running ahead every once in a while to take a particularly large stick or rock out of the way. Toward the end of the summer, we went on a weekend trip to Niagara Falls. Ali acted as the young boy's eyes, taking his arm as they walked down the path to the bottom of the falls, describing the crashing water. Looking at Ahmed, giggling with Ali as they leaned over the railing to feel the wind in their hair and the water splashing against their faces, it was hard to believe this was the same little boy I'd first seen sitting in an old wheelchair, his head bent.

Not only were my kids forming lifelong friendships with one another, but they were also beginning to connect with American children, and local schools welcomed my kids in with open arms. In the fall of 2006 the children at an elementary school in Harlem raised $1,000 in a "penny harvest" for GMRF. Ahmed, a little girl named Meghna from Nepal, and two children who had lost limbs in the 2004 tsunami in Indonesia all went to the school to thank the students, answering questions about their injuries and their cultures. I was so proud that my kids were breaking down walls between cultures, and showing American children that they were just like them. And I knew from the thank-you notes, sometimes with small donations, that I received afterward that many of the American students had gone home and told their parents about the nice kids from other countries they had met, broadening the web of compassion and understanding.

All of these connections being made seemed to be healing on

so many levels—just like when Ali read the box of letters that Lauren's friends had written on his behalf. Now, dozens of friendships were being created between kids in diverse cultures. A grassroots network of helpers from around the world, people who felt just like I did, were connecting through GMRF. And in some cases, the children themselves were healing my helpers.

A few months before Ahmed arrived for his second visit in July, I received a beautiful letter and a donation from a young veteran and artist, Aaron Hughes, who lived near Chicago. It read, in part:

> *This donation is a result of my experience in Iraq, and the pictures I draw based on my memories of the year I spent there. This is a reminder of how blessed I am to still be alive and, because of that, how much I need to give back. Elissa, I admire your ability to communicate the needs of humanity and actualize them. I am attempting to do the same with my artistic abilities . . . Thank you and GMRF for giving me a way to give back to the children in Iraq and others like them around the world.*

I called Aaron to thank him for the check and to tell him how moved I was by his stark black-and-white drawings of dusty oil fields, soldiers, and children. I could see his tortured soul in his art. Several drawings and paintings on Aaron's website depicted children, tired-looking and barefooted, with outstretched hands—as if begging—and dark haunting eyes.

"When I was deployed I lost faith in most things, and the art was something I could trust," Aaron explained, his voice so serious and yet also so soft and vulnerable. "I saw families who had lost everything, children who were starving and injured. Soldiers who were burnt-out and worse. I came home sad and bitter. Drawing and painting pictures of what I had seen and felt was a healing process."

"I know exactly what you mean," I said. Music had done the same thing for me when I came out of the darkness of losing three of the people I most loved. I felt a kinship to this young man who was obviously still grieving, the way I had for so many years.

"You know, I still see the children," Aaron said quietly. "Standing by the side of the road, begging for food. Some sitting in the dirt because they're injured and can't stand. Giving you money to heal some of these kids means a lot to me. It's like I'm also helping to give them back their lives—and that's healing for me."

Aaron and I continued to email back and forth, and he told me he was coming out to New York in the fall for two weeks, for work and vacation. I was so excited to meet him—and to introduce him to someone very special.

———

Aaron was clearly nervous the first time he met Ahmed, on the big grassy lawn behind Mount Manresa, running his hand through his short, light brown hair and licking his lips. "This is my friend, and he's your friend too," I said to Ahmed. Aaron held out his hand, which of course Ahmed didn't see, and he went right in for a hug. The anxious lines on Aaron's face melted away into a smile.

"Nice meeting you," said Ahmed, who had learned a bit of English by now. "Me Ahmed! Nice meeting you."

"Kids are so wise," Aaron said to me later that day, while we were walking around the grounds of Mount Manresa. "It was like he knew how nervous I was and he was telling me—showing me—that everything between us was cool. I'm thinking about how I can embody what he brought to that space: love and compassion—like every kid so naturally brings to a new friend."

"Trust," I said, taking Aaron's hand; he gave it a long squeeze. Aaron spent some time helping Ahmed to take photos, helping him to hold the camera up to his head and listen to the shutter click. The boy was concentrating so hard, like he was remembering when he had taken a photo and could see. There was something so hopeful about the photos Ahmed took: flashes of light in the dark night.

It was a transformational two weeks for both the young Iraqi War vet with delicate features and the little boy he helped to fly a kite, ride the subway, and run down the sidewalk while holding his hand. Ahmed trusted Aaron to be his eyes, to tell him when there was a curb to step down or that he needed to let out more string so the kite could soar into the sky. And Aaron trusted this little boy with his heart. Not long after Aaron returned to his home, he wrote me this note:

*Love, compassion, forgiveness. Meeting Ahmed was a healing moment for me. It also made me feel really committed to helping other vets who feel what I felt. I wanted to share with them that experience of knowing there's love that bonds all people, reaching far beyond being placed on different sides of the war. I began speaking to groups of vets about how the experience of being in the war doesn't need to define all of who they are, helping them to tell their stories and heal.*

I could see that while Aaron was helping to heal Ahmed, the little Iraqi boy was also helping to soothe this soldier's tortured soul. Just as Kenan had helped me. And now Aaron was also helping other emotionally injured veterans who were haunted by their memories of war. All of these people were connected in a beautiful and genuine way, broadening the circle of light that my big global family shined onto the world.

## CHAPTER SIXTEEN

# Standing Up to the Wrecking Ball

*August 2007*

In retrospect, I should have seen it coming, that big black ugly sphere swinging in slow motion right at the townhouse I had so happily shared with Asko, Kenan, and Shilo for seven years. I should have heard the crane engine revving up, the creaking metal chain hoisting that metal ball, months before.

I remember going to my father's house in New Jersey for Sunday dinner on a clear, sunny day. Maybe we'd go to the beach for sunset if dinner was over in time. Asko was behind the wheel, I was beside him, and Kenan sat in the backseat. *Ding.* I took the BlackBerry out of my purse and read the text silently, quickly. "Don't these people know it's Sunday, the day of rest?" Asko said, his voice tense.

"It's already nearly Monday morning in Iraq," I said, putting the BlackBerry back in my pocket but keeping my hand on it.

Kenan tried breaking the ice by singing, "Does anybody really know what time it is? Does anybody really care?" Neither Asko nor I were laughing, though.

"I've got two kids, Dalal and a new boy, waiting for their visas to be approved and Marla's working on airline tickets for

Friday . . ." My voice trailed off as the phone rang. I looked at Asko, as if for approval to answer it. He kept his gaze on the road, no emotion on his face. We both knew what I would do.

"Hello? Marla, did you get the tickets? Excellent!"

After I hung up, Asko kept staring straight ahead as he said, very calmly, "Can't you give it up for even a few hours with your family?"

I didn't answer, gripping the BlackBerry in my hand. I knew Asko was angry; his voice was too even, too cool. We'd had this conversation so many times during the months before Ahmed left. I was trying very hard to get him into the program for blind children for another year, and taking him to doctor appointments in the hopes he might be able to see again—just a little light even. I would cry at night, so afraid for this little blind boy. What would happen to him when he went back to living in a war zone?

"It's not like I'm insensitive to what you're doing, but there's only so much you can do," Asko had said. Of course, and I knew how much he cared—and how much he himself was doing. I always said that Kenan was the pulse of GMRF and Asko was the backbone, keeping up my website, designing brochures, driving kids to hospital appointments, fixing a leaky faucet or creaky door at Mount Loretto during the first few years he was here. He never complained that at times I spent some of my meager salary from the charity to pay for Kenan's school, send a check to Moises in South America to help support his family, or buy extra socks and a warm coat for whomever was staying at Mount Manresa at the time. And, most important, Asko was my rock, keeping me calm and steady when things became crazy busy—which was often.

"I just can't let it go, not for a day. Not even for an hour," I had said, trying to explain. "These kids—these families—are all depending on me. They've lost so much, and I'm just trying to do what I can."

"But you have to put boundaries between your private life and the charity, or one of them is going to suffer at the expense of the other."

Yes, I knew Asko was right. I should put the BlackBerry away—maybe even turn the thing off. But I needed to send a text to Mohammed at HOC, who was coordinating visas for me in Kuwait. And then send an email to the Internet café in Baghdad where Dalal's father checked in, to tell him about the travel plans so he could relay the information to the other family.

My hands were actually shaking as I typed, my breath coming faster. "I just have to send two more messages, then I'm done . . ." My voice trailed off. Even I didn't believe that. Asko was quiet; Kenan didn't even try cracking a joke. I sighed—resignation, relief, maybe even a little sadness—as I went back to attending to my emails.

———

I should have paid more attention, sooner. But by the time I saw that steel ball threatening to crash through my kitchen window, it was too late.

"Christina? It's me again."

"E, it's okay. Just take a deep breath," she said. This was the fifth time I'd called her since breakfast. It had been like this for the past two weeks as Asko seemed to be avoiding me—working late, taking Shilo for hour-long walks in the evenings, staying up late watching movies with Kenan, but I didn't hear them laughing. And he never shouted upstairs, "I love you, babe!"

"I'm trying, I'm really trying," I said, my voice cracking. "I keep asking him what's wrong and he just says 'nothing.'"

*Nothing.* The word sent a chill through me every time Asko said it, so cool and calm. Like steel.

"Did you tell him you're going to take next weekend off?" Christina asked hopefully. "That has to show him how much you care."

I'd surprised Asko with a reservation at a romantic inn for his birthday, just the two of us. I'd even leave the BlackBerry at home and Kenan would check for messages. "I told him last night, and this morning he said he doesn't want to go. He didn't give a reason. He just said he doesn't want to. C, what am I gonna do?"

"You're going to make him talk about it, get it out into the open. E, it's the only way that you two are going to work this out and save your marriage."

I knew that Christina was right. "I'll wait until tomorrow morning," I said, buying a little time. I hardly slept that night, rehearsing what I was going to say, thinking about what I was going to do differently from now on. Maybe I could leave the BlackBerry in my office during dinner, then check it quickly just after we ate and then again before bedtime. I could do that. Maybe I could leave it off while we slept.

But I knew it wasn't really just about the BlackBerry. It couldn't be just about the BlackBerry. "Asko?" I said softly when he began stirring around seven. It was early, but I couldn't wait a minute longer. "You awake?"

"I guess I am now."

"We need to talk. Really talk."

He sat up and rubbed his eyes, but didn't look at me. I grabbed his arm to get his attention. "You have to tell me what's wrong so we can fix it."

He shook his head, slowly—almost robotically. "I can't say. It's just that I don't feel it anymore," he said. *Nothing. Like steel.*

"You don't love me anymore?" I whispered, the words curling around my heart like choking vines.

"I just can't . . ."

"Can't what?"

Nothing.

"Can't what? Love me?"

*Nothing.* The silence was deafening, pounding in my temples like a bass drum.

In that moment, all of the insecurities and fears I'd fought so hard to push away—all of those years grieving, beginning when Daddy left us—came hurtling toward me, heavy and unstoppable, as if they would not just destroy my marriage and my happiness but also destroy me. I couldn't let that happen, not now. My life wasn't just about me anymore—it wasn't even about Asko and our marriage. There were now close to one hundred children depending on me to be strong so that I could help them become whole again. How could I let down these loving children and their families, who had put their trust in me?

"Get out," I said, getting out of bed, putting on my robe. Asko looked at me, maybe for the first time in weeks. I saw, reflected in his face, the pain that I felt.

*Stay, my sweet Asko, please stay. Dear God, I'm begging you. Don't leave me like everyone else I've ever loved.*

"Get out," I said again, tears streaming down my face.

Now, he was looking at me. "Elissa, no . . . Don't do this."

"If you don't love me, I don't want you here," I said. "Just go."

"I'm going to work, but we'll talk tonight," Asko said. "We'll talk, I promise."

But the truth was, it was too late for talking. The wrecking ball had been set in motion months ago, and there was no holding it back now.

———

I had no idea what I was going to do without Asko, but I knew whom to call. I'd had lots of friends during my life, lots of very good friends. But Christina knew how much I gave up for the charity, and she also understood how much I loved Asko. She was someone I didn't need to explain anything to. "E, just drop everything, get on a train, and come down here," she said. "Now."

I had Kenan drive me to Penn Station. After Asko left, I'd called Kenan at the small compnay where he did part-time computer support work. I was crying hysterically and he came home right away. At first, he couldn't believe that Asko had left me. "No, that's not right," he kept saying. "Are you sure?"

"I'm sorry," I said, seeing how hurt and confused Kenan was.

"I'm going to spend a few days with Christina so Asko can pack up his stuff. I'm sorry it has to be this way."

It was a Monday afternoon and Christina dropped everything, arranging for her husband, Larry, to take care of the kids, and taking a few days off from work even though she'd just started freelancing as an investigator for the government. "Alex and I will be okay, Mom," Lauren had reassured her. "You have to go. Elissa's your BFF—best friend forever."

Christina and I drove straight to the beach; it was two hours of laughing, crying, cursing, and a lot of singing.

I felt a little insane with the pain, thinking about how it was going to be coming home to a bedroom with empty drawers, empty closets, and a very empty bed. But I couldn't fall apart, I just couldn't. I had Kenan to think about and my work. Spending four days at the beach with my best friend—the Thelma to my Louise—was exactly what I needed.

Neither one of us had much money to spend, so we looked for the cheapest hotel on the water. It had to be on the water, that's all I cared about. We settled on a little fifties-style motel wedged between the fancy high-rise hotels and shared a room with two twin beds. It was perfect. We stayed up late talking in the pub a few doors down, me drinking beer and Christina with her usual chardonnay. We slept way into the morning and spent the afternoons walking along the beach, eating Dairy Queen soft-serve cones. I remember eating two in a row, then turning to Christina and saying, "One more, C?"

"One more," she agreed. "Whatever you need, E."

On the third night, I told Christina I was ready to go home. "It's going to be different without Asko," I said.

I sipped my margarita and shook my head. It was going to be a long time until I was ready for a new relationship. "What are you talking about? I have Kenan, I have my kids. I have you."

I raised my glass. "Here's to Thelma and Louise, going to . . . God only knows where!"

Christina clinked her glass with mine. "One thing I can guarantee: wherever you go next it's sure to be an adventure!"

## CHAPTER SEVENTEEN

# Haiti

*Port-au-Prince, February 2010*

Driving into Port-au-Prince not long after dawn, what hit me first was the smell: garbage, gasoline, and something I couldn't quite put my finger on. It was like a whiff of hamburger gone bad, magnified by 100,000. It wasn't just sickness and filth, urine and burning trash, stinging your nostrils. This was a smell that you actually feel, deep in your gut and your soul.

I had been to countries ripped apart by war—Iraq, Bosnia—but the devastation here, where Mother Nature has also acted as the enemy, was shocking and nothing short of surreal. Buildings tipped on their sides lay next to perfectly intact houses painted in bright Caribbean colors. Rubble spilled out into the heavily trafficked streets. Shiny SUVs, trucks with American, Spanish, Chinese, and French emblems, drove in a steady stream, with motor scooters and bicycles darting in and out of traffic. Ramshackle "tap-tap" buses ambled cheerily through the chaos like circus caravans, painted in wild colors with JESUS SAVES and GOD IS GRACIOUS in flowing letters along the sides.

I looked at the men, women, and children of all ages lining the narrow sidewalks littered with rubble, some squeezing into slivers of shade to escape the already blistering sun. Their dark eyes were empty, their faces drawn, their arms hanging limp by their sides. Even those selling goods on the sidewalk—a meticulous pyramid of oranges, a table piled high with tubes of toothpaste, a blanket spread with what appeared to be dozens of mismatched shoes—wore blank faces as they stood silently and waited.

Everyone seemed to be waiting. It had been a month since the 7.0 magnitude earthquake that shook the world, nearly three weeks since the 5.9 aftershock that lasted only a few seconds but had people scrambling for tap-taps out of the city. Some 20,000 people had clamored on the sandy shores as they waved their arms futily at cruise ships too far away—or too scared—to come rescue them. And more aftershocks were predicted. People were still afraid to go into what buildings remained. So, they stood instead on the sidewalks, slept in the streets, and waited. It was the children I noticed most, of course. They looked as if the life had been sucked out of them. My gaze and my heart gravitated to the young amputees, many of whom sat on blankets because there weren't even close to enough crutches, walkers, and wheelchairs to go around. When it became too painful to look at them, I closed my eyes for a moment. It was these children I was there to help, but there were so many of them. I was overwhelmed by the vision of how small I am—how small my charity is—in the face of this immense and desperate situation.

———

"We were doing thirty to a hundred amputations a day after the earthquake," a pretty blonde doctor told me as she guided me through a maze of white tents set up on the grounds of General Hospital, the largest medical facility in Port-au-Prince. "This country is going to have to figure out what to do with an entire generation of amputees."

This tent city of patients and families—hundreds of people afraid to go inside the hospital—was the same scene I'd witnessed at a half-dozen medical facilities and refugee camps during the past few days as I made my list of child amputees, just as I did in Sarajevo and Basra. But this was even worse. Never had I, nor had the world for that matter, seen so many amputees concentrated in one place. The latest estimates had put the number of earthquake casualties at 250,000, with as many as 100,000 amputees and another 50,000 who would likely need a limb amputated because of infection within the year. At least 30,000 of those amputees are children. In a country where kids ride their bikes or walk to school and church, many men are manual laborers, and women clean and cook to support their families, this constitutes a national disaster of epic proportions. Not surprisingly, there are no prostheses manufacturers in Haiti.

We weaved through row after row of white tents crammed with patients, many with bandaged heads and limbs, resting on army cots set up in the patchy grass. Family members sat in groups under trees, on the curbs, or in metal chairs set up outside the bigger tents with handmade signs: EMERGENCY ROOM, MATERNITY, ORTHOPEDICS. I took bags of nuts and crackers out of my backpack; it was touching to see how gracious and grateful people were, and painful to reach into my bag and realize it was empty.

I stopped at a tent with a young girl sitting up in bed. Her straight black hair fell against thin shoulders, and her smile was nothing short of dazzling. I walked toward her, as if pulled by a magnet. The sheets were scrunched up at the end of the bed, revealing one thin brown leg that ended in chipped pink toenails and one thigh that ended in a thick bandage above her knee.

"I'm Elissa," I said, putting my hand to my chest. I reflexively poised my pen to write down this girl's name and find out where her parents were. "Your name?"

"Claudine." The girl reached out to touch my dangling silver earrings. At the same time, I felt the doctor's hand on my arm and resisted brushing it away.

"I know," I said, giving the girl a stick of gum from my pocket and moving away, shaking off the doctor's hand as I cut our tour short. *Damn it, I know.*

It had been the same story at the four or five facilities I'd visited over the past few days, the same dead-end conversation that I had dealing with hospital administrators in Sarajevo. Some things haven't changed a bit over the past fourteen years.

Within a few minutes, while I was explaining how I want to find just a few kids to take back to New York with me so that Shriners can give them new limbs, the Partners in Health doctor was shaking her head. "What we really need is prosthetics and treatment here, organizations like Shriners to set up programs here."

I knew this was true. Dozens of organizations, along with the Haitian government, were trying to solve the biggest single medical problem resulting from the earthquake: caring for amputees. There was talk of setting up prostheses manufacturers in the country and creating clinics specifically devoted to providing physical therapy for amputees and the refitting of limbs needed as children grow. Doctors were asking charities to donate used prosthetics to hospitals in Haiti, as Princess Diana did for land mine victims. I had seen this before, the burst of fervor after a natural disaster in an underdeveloped country. And I saw in Bosnia how even well-meaning doctors and government officials lose their passion and patience when the world's short attention span shifts elsewhere and things in their country are left virtually the same. Besides, I don't have the money or the patience for long-term solutions. I see kids who have lost hope, shriveling up like the starfish on the beach, and I know I can reach out and help them to get their lives back— right now.

I took a deep breath. "Of course programs here are the goal, but I don't have that kind of money. And while you're waiting for those prostheses factories to be built and clinics to be funded, I have a real solution for a handful of kids. GMRF has helped more than one hundred kids over the past thirteen years, fitting them with prosthetic limbs and bringing them back as they grow to get refitted. Shriners are committed to these kids until age twenty-one—for free."

I had learned to wait at this point in my conversations with doctors while one of two things happen. Either I see the shaking head and the offered hand and I'm given the bum's rush out the door, as at General Hospital, or the real talking begins, like a few hours later at Love a Child, an orphanage-turned-treatment center on the border of the Dominican Republic. As

I explained GMRF's mission, the medical director's eyes lit up. "Free?" she asked. "Until they're twenty-one years old?"

"Yes and yes," I reassured her, knowing how rare both of those items are, let alone offered together.

"Look, I'm sorry for being skeptical," she said. "But during the two weeks I've been here at least a hundred people have shown up claiming to want to help the orphans here. Some of them just start walking around talking to the children, taking pictures—it's pretty clear they're not from legitimate charities. But it's hard to tell who is, and who's just trying to traffic kids."

After I showed her my website on her laptop, the medical director seemed to relax. She offered me a cup of coffee, and we sat down and started talking about how we might work together. There were a few orphans there who had lost limbs, but they weren't candidates for GMRF because they didn't have a guardian to travel with them. But there was a refugee camp attached to Love a Child that had about a dozen child amputees and their families. The medical director took a small stack of GMRF applications and said she'd talk to the parents. As I left, I told myself that it was a good meeting and at least a few applications were bound to come back to me filled out—eventually. Although, truth be told, more than a year later I was still waiting. Have I mentioned that I sometimes lack patience when it comes to helping kids?

Fortunately, I'm not the only one who has a whatever-it-takes attitude when it comes to helping a child after a natural disaster. I've hooked up with partners all over the world, like Dhyta, a New Yorker originally from Jakarta who volunteered in Indonesia after the 2005 tsunami there and emailed me about two children who needed new limbs. And Rebecca, the nurse who called me about Moises, the paralyzed boy in El Salvador. I came across some wonderful partners in Haiti too, but first I had to learn to have some patience.

———

The next trip to Haiti began when I received an email from a podiatrist volunteering at Jacmel Hospital, about thirty miles north of Port-au-Prince. She was working with a newly formed small nonprofit in Philadelphia and had identified four kids as good candidates for prosthetic limbs. But they had a problem: the American government had placed a hold on all Haitians coming to the United States for medical care or anything else. That's where I came in—getting medical visas for children, even when it seems impossible, is one thing I've mastered. So for the past few weeks I'd been texting Kathy, the podiatrist in Jacmel, to get information about the children. I also put a plan in place with Joan, the head of the charity in Philadelphia, for the children and their moms to stay at my facility in Staten Island, where I'd look after them while they were fitted for prostheses.

Now, as the car inched away from General Hospital through downtown Port-au-Prince, I was on my way to meet these particular kids, along with my friend and partner Kaveh Alizadeh, a plastic surgeon who was volunteering at a small hospital on the border of Haiti and the Dominican Republic. I stole a glance at him, sleeping next to me in the backseat of the car. He looks like a Persian George Clooney with a dash of Omar Sharif. It's his big heart that really makes him gorgeous, though. He's worked for free on several GMRF kids who had severe burns on their faces, and he'd come to Haiti to volunteer at a makeshift hospital in Jimani, a little town on the border of the Dominican Republic. He had done at least fifteen surgeries during the past two days. Now, he had volunteered to come with me on a half-day trip to Jacmel in case the kids needed a doctor during transit.

I checked my BlackBerry to make sure it was turned on: I'd been emailing back and forth for three weeks with an administrator at Homeland Security about getting humanitarian parole approved for the Haitian kids and their moms, and it was due to come through at any minute. Then Naz, a legislative assistant in Congressman Mike McMahon's office, could fax the visas here. If all went well, these kids would be among the first child amputees injured during the Haitian earthquake to receive permission to come into the United States for medical care, opening the gate for others to follow—just like Ali did for dozens of kids in Iraq.

*Ding.* I jumped and looked at my BlackBerry. "Cross your fingers," I said aloud, even though Kaveh was still sleeping soundly. It was from Sam, a volunteer EMT from New Jersey who was with the podiatrist and the kids in Jacmel. I'd had an odd feeling about this guy ever since he called me a few days ago, and it just kept getting stronger.

"Where are U?"

"On my way to U," I wrote, and waited for the ding.

"Have HP from Haiti?" Sam asked.

A huge sigh escaped as I wrote, "We still need approval from Homeland. Before Haiti signs off." This is the same thing I told Sam when he called the night before I left and asked me to fax the paperwork I'd sent to Naz, including the approval letter from Shriners. He was all excited about hooking up with some official in Jacmel who was going to sign off on humanitarian parole. That was the first phone call from him that night, and he called me "honey" one too many times in a way that made my skin crawl. I knew then I shouldn't have faxed him the papers. It was a gut feeling that was growing stronger now.

*Ding.* Another message from Sam: "Interesting."

*Interesting. What the heck does that mean?* Now, I was certifiably nervous. I couldn't help but think of the ten American missionaries who were thrown in jail a week earlier when they tried to take thirty-three orphans out of the country without the proper papers. I also couldn't help but think about the second phone call I had with Sam the night before I left for Haiti. It was one in the morning, just hours after I'd faxed him my paperwork and hours before I needed to get up for a seven forty-five flight to Santo Domingo. I was dead tired. Sam was saying something about a pilot he met who'd take the kids out of Jacmel on a private plane to Philadelphia, asking me how much I'd be willing to pay to be on board. It sure woke me up when he threw out $10,000 as a ballpark figure. No way does GMRF have that kind of funding, and this guy already knew that I had secured free flights for the children. Besides, the plan was to fly to Newark, not Philadelphia. None of this conversation was making sense—apparently, not to Sam either.

"Look, lady," he said suddenly in a pseudo Tony Soprano sneer when I declined his offer. "Whaddaya think, we're gonna pay for you to fly back with us?"

"No," I said coolly. "I think we're going to wait for humanitarian parole to come through, and then I will get myself on a flight. Good night."

Now, I was anything but cool sitting in the back of that car, dust somehow seeping through the closed windows, only a hint of cool air sifting through the air conditioner—and that smell I hadn't been able to identify when we'd first entered Port-au-Prince. I suddenly recognized it: fear.

"Did you find someone to sign off on humanitarian parole? Who?" I quickly typed into the tiny keyboard, hoping my fingers were punching approximately the right keys. I waited for a reply. Nothing. Five long, silent minutes later I sent a text to Naz for a Homeland Security update. "Nothing so far. Blizzard in D.C., so everything's closed down for the day," she wrote back.

And still not a word from Sam. I flipped through my photos for a distraction and found the one I wanted, brushing a finger gently over the round-faced boy with untamable curls and a crooked smile. Kaveh was awake now, looking over my shoulder at the BlackBerry screen. "If Kenan was here, he'd be cracking jokes like always," he said.

"Yeah, most of them about me." I smiled, thinking of how scared I had been during the six weeks before Kenan first came to Staten Island. But I was also so excited, wanting to nudge time forward to see what would come next. Exactly like I felt now, on my way to see the kids in Jacmel.

———

"E-lee-sa," Kaveh said in a teasing sing-song way that made me break my stare from the BlackBerry. "Relax," he said and gave me that George Clooney grin. "You know that everything will work out as it should. Right?"

"Yeah, right." I scowled and smiled at the same time. It had been two hours since the last text from Sam or Naz—or anyone for that matter.

We were sitting in the Plaza Hotel bar, having a Coke before we left for Jacmel. The Plaza is a dreamlike tropical fortress amidst the nightmare of Port-au-Prince. An impossibly cool breeze wafted over me as a waiter in a white jacket delivered drinks to the mahogany table overlooking an inviting turquoise pool. This is where all of the reporters stay, and we were surrounded by mostly Caucasians with American and British accents, dressed in khakis and polo shirts, tapping away at their laptops and eating burgers. I felt such guilt sitting in this haven of beauty, safety, and unlimited food.

*Ding.* I jumped, nearly spilling my Coke on the red linen tablecloth as I grabbed my BlackBerry. "It's from Betty," I told Kaveh, who nodded, knowing her name well. Betty's fifteen-year-old nephew, Tambwee, lives in the Congo, where Betty was born, and has such severe spinal deformities that he can't comfortably sit or stand. One of the Shriners met Betty through a mutual friend and asked me to make an exception for the boy.

"When does Tambwee come?" Betty had written, not for the first time during the past few weeks. I knew she was anxious, and I wished I had better news. The Congo embassy was sending me emails asking for the same information about the boy and his father that I'd already faxed four times. Unfortunately, this is not unusual. I've gone through the same scenario with Iraq, Kuwait, China, Indonesia, and Nepal.

"Y'know, Betty called me just before we came here and told me not to tell anyone Tambwee is coming," I said to Kaveh, who was oblivious that the two women at the table next to us were checking him out. "Apparently, lots of his neighbors are jealous that he's getting help in the States. She's afraid someone will put a voodoo spell on me. That's just what I need now, right?"

Kaveh laughed. "You don't believe in that stuff, do you?"

Generally, no, I'm not a big believer in voodoo or even bad luck. My experience is that God tends to test my faith, pushing me to my edge to see how far I can go—then pushes a little further.

"Well, a lot of my stuff has been disappearing," I said, mostly just to tease Kaveh. "Last night I know I put my phone recharger next to the bed and this morning it was clear across the room on the floor, along with the protein bars that were in my suitcase."

"That's not so surprising considering how little sleep you've been getting, and the stress you're under," responded the ever-logical doctor.

"Maybe," I said, sending Sam yet another text asking if he was going to be at the hospital in an hour when we got to Jacmel. What I hadn't told Kaveh is what really had my stomach in knots: A few weeks ago, I had gone to see a woman whom I guess you could call a seer. My friend Margaret, who's from Santo Domingo, swore that Grace was the real deal. I'd been so worried about the charity, with the economy tanking over the past year and donations practically nil. Plus, Kenan had graduated from college last fall and needed a full-time job by July to get a work visa. Neither one of us could envision him going back to Bosnia; his home and his life were in New York now.

Grace was a lovely spiritual woman, and I'd decided she was, at the very least, highly perceptive. I hadn't heard from her since that time several weeks ago when she'd lit ten pink candles and read my cards along with the bubbles in little glass bowls of water. She saw me in a big house with a fountain and four cars—you gotta love that! And this was spot on: she saw me as a mermaid in my past life.

It was three in the morning before my flight to Haiti when I answered my phone. "Elissa, are you going to Haiti?" Grace asked in her thick, rich Dominican accent.

"Sure, in a few hours," I said, a little freaked out. I hadn't told her about my trip.

"Please, you must come here now. I had a vision of someone who wants to do you harm. But don't worry, I have an ankle bracelet I've blessed to ward off this evil."

"Voodoo?" I asked groggily, thinking of the warning I'd had from Betty. "Someone from the Congo or Haiti?"

"No, not voodoo, but someone means to do you harm. You must be wary of an American man with blond hair."

At the time, I wasn't concerned enough to hightail it up to Grace's apartment in the Bronx. But now, I asked one of the women at the table next to us if I could borrow her laptop for a minute. I Googled Sam and hit a link to his professional website: sure enough, there was a photo of a guy who had thick, blond hair.

———

I wasn't really surprised—more relieved—when the phone rang a few minutes after Kaveh and I got back into that hot stuffy car heading toward Jacmel. It was Bob, a GMRF board member and head of Shriners volunteer transportation unit—a real sweetheart of a guy.

"Stop the car," I said to our driver. He pulled over as I finished my phone conversation. I felt all of the emotion that had been churning up in me, the anxiety that had been building since the phone calls with Sam the night before leaving for Haiti draining from my body as Bob spoke. I had been waiting for another shoe to drop and this was it: It turns out that Sam had used the paperwork I'd filled out for humanitarian parole and, without my permission or knowledge, gotten the kids visas through another route in Haiti that was faster than slow-moving Homeland Security. Naz later told me that humanitarian parole can sometimes be obtained through the U.S. Border Patrol, and Sam apparently had some connections he wasn't telling me about.

Bob told me that Joan, the head of the charity Sam volunteers with, had called Shriners Children's Hospital of Philadelphia not long before that to tell them the kids were on their way, in a private jet. It turns out that, all along, they'd been making plans for the kids to stay in private homes in Philadelphia instead of with me on Staten Island. I didn't have problems with any of those details, only that they hadn't been straight with me. I would have gotten the humanitarian parole for them anyway. Never mind that now I was somewhere in Haiti on my way to . . . nowhere.

At least, that's what I thought at the time.

———

On the car ride back to Good Samaritan Hospital, the small hospital in Jimani where Kaveh was volunteering, I pretended to sleep so that I wouldn't have to show my mixed emotions. On the one hand, I was truly relieved that the four kids in Jacmel that I'd spent the past three weeks securing humanitarian parole for were on their way to Philadelphia. But I was also sick to my stomach thinking about how this charity I'd thought was my partner on this mission had used me to get what they needed. I was more sad than angry, and not really all that surprised. The competition for funding and resources among small charities—people with basically good intentions all working toward the same goal—can be fierce, and, unfortunately, it can get nasty. The trick is to keep the faith anyway, because the vast majority of the other small charities I hook up with are right on the same page with me. Maybe they weren't working out of their walk-in closets, but they were honest and meant only to do as much good as they could.

Kaveh tried consoling me. "I know your heart was set on helping those kids in Jamal, but there are others."

I sighed. The sad truth of it was that there were always others. I had a folder overflowing with requests for kids from Iraq and other countries on the desk in my office. "It's just that I really wanted to help after the earthquake, give some hope to a country that's in such desperate need. Like you are at the hospital."

"Well," Kaveh said, "there are two girls at Good Samaritan who each lost an arm."

Two days earlier, when I'd arrived in Jimani, I'd spent lots of time talking to volunteers and visiting with the thirty or so recovering children in the makeshift treatment center. Surely I'd have noticed two amputees. "Really?" I asked.

"I operated on one of them," Kaveh said. "They both had gangrene. Their bandages had obviously been on for two weeks, since the earthquake, and were incredibly dirty and worn. It's a tragedy, knowing that their arms could have been saved if they had gotten to us earlier."

By the time we returned to Jimani, the sun was setting behind the mountains that cradle Good Samaritan Hospital. At first glance, this could have been an old southern plantation home with its sturdy white columns and big wraparound porches. The second-story veranda even has rocking chairs that overlook the pristine Lago del Fondo, which separates the Dominican Republic from Haiti. Then, your eyes travel down to the big dusty yard with a half-dozen large tents pitched to one side where patients are recovering, and small tents in another cluster where volunteers from the United States and Spain sleep. A big *X* is painted in the dust where helicopters sometimes land, and wounded patients are unloaded onto stretchers from two trucks parked at the front doors. During the first few weeks after the earthquake, mattresses with patients lined the hospital hallways and spilled outside onto the porch and yard.

Now, I knew this was my last night in Haiti: there was no reason to stay since the kids in Jacmel had already left for Philadelphia. And I was tired of waiting around to ask, yet again, for someone's permission to offer help. Honestly, after the day I'd had, I was too tired for another round of explanations and I couldn't handle another rejection.

I walked out the front door, heading toward the pediatric tents one last time. The greatest sound hit my ear as I came closer: a boom box blasting Michael Jackson's "Billie Jean" mixed with the laughter of children. Suddenly, I wasn't tired at all; I remembered why I was here. Some of the kids were dancing with their parents and Peace Corps volunteers, while others looked on from their beds. A volunteer took my hand and we slowly danced in a circle with a young boy whose arm was in a sling. This was the happiest I'd been all day. God bless the healing power of music.

The song ended and I heard Kaveh calling my name. "Where have you been?" he asked, breathless, pulling me away. "Never mind, this way."

We stopped at a tent toward the back of the property and Kaveh stepped inside, smiling triumphantly. "This is Margarette. She's seventeen," Kaveh said, holding out his arm toward a cot where a thin dark-skinned girl was lying, her arm amputated above the elbow and bandaged.

"*Bonjour,*" I said, kneeling beside the cot. Margarette was curled into herself against the thigh of her father, who sat on her bed. Servius looked briefly at Kaveh and me, then back down to continue stroking the thick braids on the girl's head. She glanced at me, then away. I recognized the look: trauma, shock, mistrust.

Kim, a nurse I'd met before, was changing the girl's IV bag. "Margarette was in school when the earthquake happened and four hundred children died," Kim explained. "She was holding her best friend's hand, and they were both crushed. The doctors saved her friend's arm, but . . ."

"I'm so sorry," I said, wishing I knew even a little French. As I held out my hand to Servius, it struck me that this was the first time all day that I was actually meeting a parent of a child who needed a new limb. "I'm going to help," I said, hoping that he believed me.

"Let me try," Kim said, then spoke fluently in French for a few minutes. Servius looked at me, incredulous. I recognized this look too. I nodded vigorously, smiling. "How do you say 'it's true'?" I asked Kim as I reached out my hand to Servius.

"*Il est vrai,*" she said. Servius smiled broadly, but his daughter continued to stare blankly. It would take time, I knew. And that was okay. For some things, I can be very patient.

## CHAPTER EIGHTEEN

# No Coincidences

꩜

❧ One thing I've learned over fourteen years of running GMRF is that there are no coincidences. People seem to show up when they're supposed to, where they're supposed to, so I try to look around and pay attention. I forgot, for a moment, to do that in Haiti, and I nearly missed Margarette. That evening there was a prayer circle of patients and volunteers in the field behind the hospital. I watched from the second-floor veranda, leaning over the railing to listen to the soft murmur of praise, picking out what sounded like French, Spanish, and English. Margarette was standing in between her father and a fair-skinned woman who was helping her to lift her arms to the sky as the setting sun turned the clouds purple against the craggy brown mountains in the distance. This woman, a doctor from Albuquerque, New Mexico, was one of those right-time right-place people, but I wouldn't know that until months later. At the time, watching her, I thought how kind she seemed. I said my own private prayer of thanks that this sweet girl had people to watch over her while she waited to get her new arm, also asking for the strength and perseverance it would no doubt take to bring her to Staten Island. I'd been through this before, the process of trying to get a child out of a country steeped in chaos.

The process was actually even more complicated than it had been to get Ali to the United States for medical care. For starters, Iraq and every other country I've dealt with have had one-page medical visa applications. But with Haiti, Christina and I spent nearly two months dealing with three different government agencies—the U.S. embassy and the Haitian Ministry of Health in Port-au-Prince, and Homeland Security here—to fill out six sets of eighteen-page applications, one each for Margarette and Servius, and separate ones for two other girls and their guardians. Chantal, age seventeen, had also had an arm amputated at Good Samaritan. She was trapped when the hotel where she worked cleaning rooms collapsed around her. Margarette and Chantal became inseparable friends while recuperating at the hospital and while sharing a tent in a refugee camp just outside of Port-au-Prince for a month. It made sense to bring the two girls to the United States together.

The other girl I was working to bring to Staten Island was eight-year-old Sarah, who had been trapped under the rubble that was once her home, for three days after the earthquake, losing both her mother and her leg. She came to me through another small NGO in Minneapolis, No Time for Poverty. My experience with them was so very different than what I had gone through with Sam. Henry, an engineering student who's also a coordinator for NTFP, helped me to get the girls out of the country, and he's now my liaison on the ground there, referring more children who need limbs and coordinating the in-country details—from obtaining medical records to making airport runs. I couldn't do what I do in Haiti without him.

I also had a lot of help from the Homeland Security office, emailing back and forth for two months with an officer named Cris, who processed the forms for each of the girls and their guardians. I had a lot of questions and wanted to make sure I had all of the details right. Along with the usual travel and medical documents there were some additional special circumstances. None of the girls had birth certificates, so their parents—or in Sarah's case her father—had to write a sworn statement stating their age and where they were born. This wasn't easy with all of the government offices still shut down after the earthquake.

By the time Christina and I went to Port-au-Prince in late April to pick up the girls and their guardians and accompany them on their first plane trip anywhere, we were confident that we'd jumped through all of the necessary hoops—right until we arrived at the check-in gate at the airport.

"You're not going anywhere," a dour-looking government official said, her arms crossed.

"Is there a problem?" I asked, racking my brain for what I could have missed. Homeland Security and the U.S. embassy had already approved all of the paperwork.

"Our Ministry of Health needs a letter from a doctor verifying that they are amputees and need prosthetic limbs."

I couldn't believe it. The girls were standing right in front of her, Sarah on one leg, leaning on crutches. Margarette and Chantal both wore short sleeves that clearly revealed their missing arms.

"Can I call the hospital and have a doctor fax the form?" I asked, trying to keep my voice calm for the sake of the girls.

"It will take three days to process," the official said flatly.

The plane was scheduled to leave in fifteen minutes—with or without us on it. Christina broke down in tears, and I had to walk away because I was so angry. Luckily, Henry was parked just outside. I had him come back in to explain to the girls and their mothers what had happened and take them back to their homes. "It's okay, Elissa. We know you'll return," they assured me, patting my back and my arm as I headed onto the plane, feeling sick to my stomach with anger and guilt. How could I have missed something? Henry took the girls to a doctor to get the additional form needed for them to board a plane with me when I returned the next week.

Christina and I were both so excited when all three of the girls finally arrived in New York on May first. At the same time, it was a bittersweet joy: we knew that eventually the girls would have to return to the country where they'd lost so much.

*August 2010*

Sarah, a petite girl with cocoa skin and eyes that are both dark and filled with light, leaned over a young boy lying on the couch in the GMRF playroom at Mount Manresa, a tube in his throat so he could eat and tubes coming out of his head to drain the excess fluid, bandages on his cheeks. It didn't matter to Sarah how Waad looked; she held a toy stethoscope to his chest. "Hmmm . . . very good," she said in a too-deep voice, mimicking the doctors she'd seen do this so many times. Both of the children were giggling, even though Waad's face was so badly scarred that he hadn't been able to smile in more than a year. The eight-year-old Iraqi boy had lost an eye, his leg, and an arm while playing with friends, when he absentmindedly kicked a can that turned out to be a grenade.

Waad was just beginning his recovery process and had already been fitted for a prosthetic arm and eye. He had to lie still after recent plastic surgery to fix his toes, which were fused together from being burned, and saline balloons were inserted into his cheeks to stretch his skin and give him back his smile. Sarah knew some of what Waad was going through. She had come over in May and was already walking on her new leg. But their relationship seemed to be about more than just this little girl encouraging a friend. They were like kindred spirits who share a special bond. Sarah taught Waad some Creole, and he taught her some Arabic words as they sat together for hours at a table in the garden at Mount Manresa. Sometimes they played cards; sometimes they just looked at each other, exchanging a smile or out-and-out cracking up. It was as if each actually knew what the other was thinking.

There are no coincidences; these two children seemed to reach out to each other and complete each other's healing process. It was the same way with Margarette, who lost her right arm, and Chantal, who lost her left arm. The two young women helped each other to get dressed in the morning and fix each other's hair; one carried a tray at breakfast while the other filled two plates with food. Another happy coincidence was that Tambwee, who did eventually come from the Congo with his father, knew French and could act as my translator with the Haitian girls. He was so sweet with Sarah, pushing her wheelchair and sometimes carrying her before she was fitted with her new leg. They all fit together like puzzle pieces during the summer months they shared together here. They became a family.

Some of my favorite moments during the months with these kids from around the globe had been in my van, on the way to Shriners Children's Hospital in Philadelphia for doctor appointments, or maybe to the zoo for an outing. We'd talk and sing in French, Arabic, Creole, English, a little Bosnian when Kenan was driving—somehow, we all understood each other. And there was a lot of laugher, the universal language. Not only did it bring all of these kids from different countries closer together, but it was also healing for both them and their guardians. Recently, we'd all been in the van—Waad and the three Haitian girls, Grace, a boy from the Congo, and all of their guardians. Kenan was driving, and Waad was watching him so carefully, leaning over his shoulder. "He's a good driver," I said. "But not always. One time, Kenan almost drove into the ocean with fishes!" I sucked in my cheeks, making my version of a fish face, and even the kids who didn't understand what I was saying laughed.

"Remember that?" I said to Kenan. I used to sit in the passenger seat, my foot against an imaginary brake on the floor, while he practiced driving around the big parking lot at the Staten Island boardwalk for hours. That was the summer when he was eighteen, determined to learn to drive before Miralem came for a visit.

"Hey, that's not fair—I was just learning," Kenan said. "And I had you as my teacher!"

"Bad teach?" Waad said, laughing, patting my shoulder.

"No, not Elissa," Margarette chimed in, she and Chantal both coming to my defense. "Elissa very smart!"

That seemed like another lifetime, back when I was afraid to drive on the highway and Kenan was the one who gave me the courage to try again. Now, Kenan was driving on his own to a part-time job as a computer technician working for Kaveh, and he had a girlfriend who was crazy about him. He had a full life and didn't consider that any kind of miracle. It was just normal. I had the same hopes for all of the children in the van.

"Wait, stop the car!" I said, spotting a mailbox at the corner. "I need to get a letter in the mail."

I gave the letter to Waad's mother, Waffa, who was sitting in the front seat next to Kenan. "Can you get out and mail this?" I asked. She nodded and took the letter, but stayed in the car, looking out the window.

"Just put it in the box," I said, thinking it might have been easier to ask Margarette, who was sitting next to me, to get out so I could mail the letter. Waffa got out of the car and looked at the blue tin box. "Open," I repeated, pantomiming pulling the slot open.

Waffa walked all the way around the mailbox, not seeing the slot on the side. She tapped on the top. "Open," all of the kids were now chanting, laughing so loud that other cars were slowing down to look at us. Waad was laughing so hard that tears came to his eyes.

"You get out, help," I told him.

The boy who couldn't smile just a month ago went to give his mother a hug and a grin, taking the letter from her and putting it into the box. Waffa covered her mouth and giggled—which just made us all crack up again. Then, we all gave her a rousing round of applause and she took a gracious bow.

Now, I watched Sarah holding Waad's hand as he drifted off to sleep. "Don't worry, Waad, don't worry," she repeated, one of the English phrases they both understand, then gently kissed her friend's hand. Waffa and Fabian, Sarah's father, were sitting nearby. When we were flying back from Haiti along with the others, I explained that they would be staying at Mount Manresa with a boy from the Congo and two Iraqi kids. "Iraq very bad," Fabian had said, pulling a face. "The people do bad things and fight."

"No, Fabi," I said. "War is bad but the people are good. Most of the people there hate the fighting and want it to stop."

Seeing is definitely believing. During the past month, Fabian had become close with Waad's mother, the two of them sitting together, occasionally sharing a smile and a few words as they watched the children. They have slowly become friends through the common bond of the children they love. Now, Waffa hugged the younger woman's shoulder. "Sarah, good girl."

"Thank you," Fabian said, hugging Waffa in turn. "Waad too, he friend. Thank you."

When Waad and the Haitian girls parted ways a few weeks later, everyone was in tears as we said our good-byes.

*September 2010*

Andrea Lill, a doctor I had met in Haiti who had also met Margarette, had been texting me for months, asking about Margarette's recovery and planning their reunion. Now, she was on her way to Staten Island for the weekend, to ask Margarette and her father a life-changing question: What would the young woman think of continuing her education in Albuquerque?

It was an amazing offer from the doctor of internal medicine: a room in her home and classes at the nearby community college. At the same time, for me it was bittersweet. I couldn't imagine separating Margarette and Chantal. And then there was Sarah, who was returning to Haiti to live in a shack just feet from where her mother died. Before they came to the United States, she and Fabian had been living in a tent made of tarps and cardboard in front of what had once been their house. Henry told me that Sarah's mother's body was still lying on a cement platform among the fallen beams that used to be their home because nobody had come to retrieve it yet.

———

Andrea arrived at Mount Manresa close to midnight and was surprised to see Margarette and Chantal waiting up for her. "Welcome," Margarette said, hugging Andrea like she was an old friend.

"Hungry?" Chantal asked, then turned to Margarette, speaking quickly in Creole, even before Andrea answered. The girls took Andrea into the dining room and disappeared into the kitchen, coming back a few minutes later with a cup of tea, bread, and peanut butter.

"For you, Mama," Margarette said. Andrea knew that this was a term of endearment and respect commonly used by children in Haiti, yet there was a warm twinge in the doctor's chest. She and her husband, who had two biological teenage daughters and an adopted special needs five-year-old son, had been talking about adopting another child from Haiti. She had gone to volunteer at

Good Samaritan for two weeks with the idea of finding a needy child to adopt. The evening I first saw Andrea in the prayer circle, helping Margarette to hold her hands up to the sky in praise of God, she had an epiphany: There were no children here to adopt, but this was the girl she'd been sent to Haiti to watch over.

Chantal didn't remember Andrea, who had changed her bandages and examined her arm after the amputation, but there was an immediate and strong bond between them. "Good?" Chantal asked as Andrea sipped her tea.

"Very good, thank you," Andrea answered, lifting her cup toward the girls. They were looking at her, talking to each other.

"You, tired," Margarette said, getting up and taking Andrea by the arm. Chantal picked up her small suitcase, refusing to let Andrea take it as the girls led her upstairs to her room.

The next day when I came to Mount Manresa after breakfast, Andrea and all three of the Haitian girls were waiting for me in the front yard. Margarette and Chantal were sitting on either side of the doctor and Sarah was in her lap. "How can I take Margarette without Chantal?" Andrea asked. I smiled shaking my head, knowing what was coming next.

"And Sarah . . ." Andrea sighed. "I just called my husband to ask if we have room for all of the girls, and Fabian, to stay at our house for awhile. How could I not help them all?"

*How could I not help?* I knew exactly how Andrea felt.

*March 2011*
*Dearest Mother,*
*We celebrate Sarah's birthday last night with many people. She is very happy with school and new home. But she say she miss*

*Waad. Chantal and me still live together in apartment near school. We enjoy classes, both think to be nurse someday. We go to Mom Andrea house many times for dinner and play with children. They our family, and you.*

           *Love,*

                *Margarette*

## CHAPTER NINETEEN

# New Beginnings

*December 25, 2011*

"I have so much to be thankful for," I say, lifting my glass of orange juice, looking around the table, and counting my blessings on Christmas morning.

I had bought this big butcher block table at a garage sale, imagining the worn wood steeped in its own history of holiday celebrations, family dinners, maybe a mother and her daughters talking over coffee in the morning. It's the first—and only—piece of furniture in this modest split-level house I purchased just weeks ago. There's a beautiful sign that sits on the front lawn as well as a plaque alongside the front doorway proclaiming it THE DARE TO DREAM HOUSE. Three angel donors—Miles Nadel; his company, MDC Partners; and celebrity Tyler Perry—made this new home for GMRF possible. While I'll always be thankful to Mount Loretto and Mount Manresa, as well as the Ronald McDonald House on Long Island, for years I've been dreaming of having a home all our own for my kids and their family members.

"Here's to being together, to family," Kenan says, and the clinking of glasses is like music. "Now, let's dig in—I'm starving!"

I look across the table at Rita Lu, who's sitting between her two grown sons, and we keep our juice glasses raised for an extra moment. *Here's to Mommy,* I think, knowing my sister is sharing my thoughts. Our mother would have been so happy to see the family sitting around this table.

So many dreams are coming true this Christmas, right here and now, around this weathered table. Miralem and Aida are visiting together for the first time; Kenan hasn't seen both of his parents since he visited Bosnia four years ago. The Malkics keep beaming at their son, who's recently been hired full-time as a computer technician at a large financial institution. And Asko is sitting beside me. He never really left my life, but this is the first holiday we've spent together in more than five years.

"To new beginnings," Asko says quietly, while everyone else is filling their plates with the scrambled eggs, fruit, and cinnamon coffee cake that Aida made. I think that only I hear Asko's toast, but Aida gently nudges me on my other side.

"I want you to be happy, Elissa," Aida had said a few weeks earlier. "When you are with him, you smile more."

"To new beginnings," I say, squeezing Asko's hand. A fresh start. A new chapter.

And here's to the many new chapters of GMRF: stories that are in the process of unraveling in wonderful ways, and stories that have only just begun.

One story began with Aurelia Curtis, who was a teacher at Curtis High School on Staten Island for more than twenty years before becoming the principal in 2003. She has never forgotten growing up near Monrovia, Liberia, against the peaceful backdrop of the Atlantic Ocean and Mount Nimba, the highest mountain in the region. She left her country in 1980 to attend Columbia University's Graduate School of Education with the thought of returning to Liberia and bettering the lives of the young people there. But then civil war broke out in the early 1990s, and Aurelia made a life for herself here, falling in love with her husband, Al, and raising two daughters on Staten Island.

Aurelia and Al, who has held several positions in New York City mayor Rudy Giuliani's administration, have been big supporters of GMRF over the past several years. When the Haitian girls were here during the summer of 2010, they took them, along with the two children from Iraq and the boy from the Congo to their church, introducing the children one by one and telling their stories. The church raised more than $2,000 to pay for clothing and whatever else the kids needed during their stay. Shortly thereafter, Aurelia went to Liberia, and a friend introduced her to Ammie, a sixteen-year-old double amputee who had recently been the victim of a hit-and-run.

"How could I not help?" Aurelia asked me when she called to tell me about Ammie, a bright girl who dreams of growing up to start her own business instead of selling trinkets on the roadside in front of her house, like her mother.

"And then once I helped one girl, more just seemed to show up," Aurelia continued excitedly.

"And they'll keep on coming as long as you're willing to help," I said. "Trust me on this."

Five children from Liberia will come to stay at the new Dare to Dream House in early 2012, and Aurelia is getting more requests daily, keeping a list, just like I did when I first went to

Bosnia, then Iraq, then Haiti. Just like I'll do when I go to Tibet and India in spring 2012—and for the rest of my life.

———

As the stories keep unfolding, my global family keeps growing, and the bridges across the globe are becoming stronger and stronger. Shortly before that Christmas morning when Asko and I reunited, I sat in an elementary school auditorium filled with hundreds of children—black, white, Asian, Arab—I couldn't have been more proud. "PS 22 and GMRF are both part of the same Staten Island community," I told the students. "Together, we reached across the world to offer a helping hand to a little girl in Libya. Malak is my hero, and you are all her heroes."

Just eight months earlier, in the spring of 2011, the children at PS 22 had raised close to $5,000. These are kids from diverse economic backgrounds, some whose parents have lost their jobs in the economic recession. And yet most of them donated at least a few dollars. Now, I'm here to show them the end result: five-year-old Malak, whose home in Misrata was hit by a missile at around the same time as the school's fund-raising carnival, hoists herself out of a wheelchair with the help of her mother. The little girl with long dark pigtails and a dimpled smile waves shyly. She doesn't know exactly what I am saying, but she surely understands the applause, whistles, and cheers filling the room.

Malak came to me through Jan Innes, whose fiancé, Ahmed, is volunteering in Misrata. The surgeon from Cairo had seen a lot since he'd first come to Benghazi in February 2011 to stitch up civilians and soldiers rebelling against Muammar Gaddafi's regime. When the fighting heated up there, he moved on to

Misrata, working in a makeshift ER in a hospital parking lot. "Ahmed has operated on other wounded children before," Jan told me in one of our early conversations, "but none as young or as traumatically wounded as Malak. The decision to amputate her leg was inevitable, but it was incredibly difficult, knowing there are no prosthetics available in Libya."

Jan, who lives in Boston, fell in love with Ahmed, a Facebook friend through a mutual acquaintance, while the two of them worked to find help for this little girl who had lost her leg and both of her younger siblings in the grenade attack. *You are my angel, the bright spot in a very dark time*, Ahmed wrote to Jan before he operated on Malak. It seemed like fate that they should help this little girl, whose name means angel in Arabic. The couple is hoping that Malak will walk down the aisle and be the flower girl at their wedding in May 2012.

As I sat in the front row of the PS 22 auditorium, Malak on one side of me and Abdeen, a four-year-old boy from Iraq, on the other side, the PS 22 chorus came on stage to sing a song that I co-wrote, "Back Together Again," to raise awareness for GMRF:

*Put them back together again.*
*Celebrate all of the miracles,*
*do everything we can.*
*Put them back together again.*
*All of the love we can give them*
*we hold safely in our hands.*

Abdeen walks up to the stage, mesmerized by the young singers, and Malak is humming along by the second round of the chorus. I take her hand, swinging it back and forth. I smile, imagining her walking down the aisle at Jan and Ahmed's wedding next spring as planned, wearing a long pink dress, barrettes gently pulling her curls off her face. I picture this beautiful little girl walking slowly, haltingly, sprinkling rose petals in front of her with one hand, the other hand holding on to my arm.

The PS 22 chorus is now singing their theme song, "Don't Stop Believin'" by Journey, and the entire auditorium is on its feet, clapping and singing along. Little Abdeen is twirling in front of the stage, fully immersed in the music. I look at Malak, as I sing along with the chorus, swept away in the music and the love in this room.

―――

I was recently asked by the Salvation Army to be part of their annual holiday drive. A few days before Christmas, on a cold and frosty morning, six of us stood ringing bells inside the Staten Island Ferry terminal as people with tired, stressed faces occasionally dropped some change or a few dollars into our big red buckets. I started humming "Jingle Bells" and tapping my feet—mostly because I was freezing—and then an idea came to me: "What we need is Christmas carols, some music to warm up everyone's hearts." So, at seven thirty in the morning we started singing: "Dashing through the snow . . ."

The effect was immediate: busy commuters slowed down to give us a smile, some singing along as they slipped a donation in the bucket. And then more people started gravitating toward the sound of singing and jingling bells. For a few moments they forgot about their desks piled with work to finish before taking a few days off for the holiday and unfinished shopping lists, and were swept into the true spirit of Christmas. I'm betting that spirit of goodwill lasted well into the day for many of those people. And who knows how many people they, in turn, made smile.

As I stood in the terminal ringing my bell, singing "Joy to the World" loud and strong, I thought about the story of the starfish thrower, tossing one bright starfish after another back into the water. I thought about the ripple effect that happens when a few people stand outside singing, and then a few more people join in the chorus. I thought about how a classroom of kids each donated fifty cents or a dollar of their allowance—and asked their parents to maybe donate a few more dollars—to help a little girl from Libya who needed a new leg. I thought about a mother and school principal who visited her homeland in Africa and wound up enlisting her church and friends to help three, then five, and quite possibly more injured children who had lost hope.

Can you imagine if we each threw back just one starfish, and maybe asked a friend or two to do the same? The shore would be a ribbon of pure inspiration. If you think about it, there are actions we can all take in our daily lives to help others in need and create a global family. I'm not talking about quitting your job, traveling across the globe, and turning your bedroom closet into an office. But sometimes we all get so busy with our lives that we place a barricade around us: a wall of *I can't, I don't have time, I can't afford it.* If you think about it, who really doesn't have time to give someone a smile? Listening to someone's worries for a few moments or saying a prayer doesn't cost a cent.

There are dozens of little things we can do in our everyday lives that add up, make a difference, and actually put a smile on our own faces!

Who knows where these small actions and a greater awareness will lead. You may find yourself, just like I've found myself, in exactly the right place at the right time to do something bigger than you ever could have imagined you were capable of accomplishing. And instead of quietly thinking *I can't*, you'll find yourself shouting: "How could I not?" ✍

# ACKNOWLEDGMENTS

Thank you. *Hvala. Tenki. Dankie. Dhanyavaad. Merci. Grazie. Ahsante sana. Do jeh. Terima kasih banyak. Tashakor. Shukran.*

To Jennifer Haupt: After writing many magazine articles about my work and the growing number of children being helped, you came to me and said, "You really need to tell your story in a book." And so . . . I talked and you wrote, and I talked some more, and we both cried and laughed. And together we created this book. You reached deep into my head and under my skin, and into my heart. To my dear friend Jen, who now knows me better than most, thank you for appreciating what it is I have chosen to do with my life and helping to give me the insight to share what I've learned with the world. I love you, my friend.

Thanks to the many people who made this book possible. Carrie Thornton: It's because of your interest in my story that it is now bound into this book. Thank you, my new and beautiful friend. David Patterson, my eloquent agent, thank you, as well as Stephanie Abou and everyone else at Foundry Literary Agency. Jessica Horvath, Christine Ball, and the marketing team at Dutton: Thank you for supporting this book. And thanks to Natalie Mines for helping to spread the word. And speaking of spreading the word, nobody deserves more thanks in that arena than Scott Pelley and the *60 Minutes* crew. Your broadcast on our work was a gift from God, and I will be forever grateful.

I want to acknowledge the many dedicated people who have helped and who continue to help make the work of GMRF possible. I apologize in advance if I have forgotten anyone, because so many have given so much of their talent, time, resources, ideas, and encouragement every day. I am honored to know and work with all of you, and I thank all of you.

To Shriners Hospitals for Children: You are GMRF's lifeline. Without you, there is no GMRF. It's as simple as that! Some of my other key medical partners are: Kaveh Alizadeh, MD, MSC; Michael Dowling, CEO of NSLIJ-Long Island Jewish Medical Center; Winthrop-University Hospital on Long Island; Dr. Pamela Gallin, Mission: Restore; and Annette Krishoff, Ocular Prosthetics. Thank you all for donating your skills to give dignity back to a child.

Miles Nadal, founder, chairman, and CEO of MDC Partners, what can I say. You are an extraordinary man. Thank you for the GMRF "Dare to Dream" house, the playground, and so, so much more that you have donated. Thanks also to Tyler Perry for your generous donation toward purchasing the "Dare to Dream" GMRF house. You are truly a selfless, genuine person.

Ronald McDonald Houses, I can never thank you enough, especially the Long Island RM House, where my kids stayed while waiting for our GMRF "Dare to Dream" house to be ready. Matt Campo, you and your staff are nothing shy of wonderful. Before we had our own house, Mount Loretto gave us our first home, and then Fr. Edward J. Quinnan gave my kids shelter at Mount Manresa when they needed it most.

I also want to thank Ambassador Muhamed Sacirbey for handing me the first starfish. You have taught me many things and have enriched my life. And Boro Vukadinovic, you are always there for me, in times of joy and in times of need. You never asked or needed to be recognized for all the kids you enabled us to help. You always did it from your heart. Know that I love you.

Thanks also to the past and present outstanding GMRF board

members: Kaveh Alizadeh; Robert Civello; Alfred Curtis (meeting you the same day I was handed Kenan's letter is no coincidence); Christina Frank; Peter Guirguis; Donna Jungreis; Daniel Kennedy; Rita Kornfeld; Bob Martin (bless your big heart, always there for me and my kids); Anne Reingold; Mohammed and Susan Sacirbey; Patrick Minter, deputy chief of the U.S. Customs and Border Protection at JFK International Airport; Carol Williamson, our angel; Larry Fischer at Viamedia; George Bleimann, my accountant whose guidance has been invaluable since day one; Jim Dawson and Seth David Walter, my genius music partners and friends; Kim Seggio, for believing in my mission every step of our fourteen years; Richmond County Savings Foundation, thank you for appreciating my mission and being the first from the financial community to help fund GMRF; Tony Burke, thanks for believing in my mission; "L" Foundation, you continue to be the biggest gift of all; Tom Roche, Church of the Resurrection, and everyone in the Rye, New York, community. Wayne Harris, you jumped in to volunteer and found yourself head-deep as part of the crew in this great journey.

Danny Carriage, I have you to thank for asking me to write the song "Let's Do a Miracle." You are my dear friend, and you are a part of that miracle. Dr. Bhupathi, thank you for saying "Yes, I want to help this boy." John DePierro, for being there from day one. Verrazano Moving, bless your charitable heart for saving the day over and over again. Bill D'Ambrosio, thank you for never doubting me. You are the epitome of humanity at its best. Maureen Seaberg, thanks for suggesting that I contact the Bosnian ambassador when I first wanted to help Bosnian children. Mrs. Callahan, my third grade teacher, I know you are smiling down on me!

To my family, I love all of you dearly: Rita Lu Kornfeld, my sister, you are my Rock of Gibraltar. Your wisdom and calm and unwavering support has confidently navigated me through my mission in which I know you mirror. Monique Montanti, my sister, for always offering to help in any way you could. Dr. Montanti, my uncle Vincent, my godfather, and Aunt Monique, bless you for all of your love and unwavering support. Mimi, my cousin, thank you for always being on top of things. Maria Montanti, you are a superwoman! Cousin Rita, the memories we share are some of the best I've lived. Aunt Tessie, Mommy's dearest and best friend. Know I love you all.

And I am blessed with some amazing friends. My dear friend of forty-something years, Donna Jungreis: I love you more than T.B.O.J.I.T.W! You are a true blessing to me and the kids. Christina Frank, you are my Thelma, my BFF, my second set of eyes and hands while traveling to countries to bring children back. You are my soul mate! Aida and Miralem Malkic, you may as well be my own blood relatives—that's how much I love you. V, you have been my right hand. Claire, you've been there since my sand castle days and always by my side. Michelle, Anthony, Kathy, it's another book. Thank you all for your loyalty. I love you. Thank you, Al and Jackie Lambert, Dr. Ahmed, and Jan Radwan for caring as you do. Uday, you are my Superman. I love you.

Thanks to my childhood friends: Bobby Jackson, who has passed on; Frankie Cianchetta and Sallie Vasile, who remain as close to me now as in my "Darla" *Little Rascals* days. I love you guys deeply, now as then.

Kenan, you have given me the greatest gift of all: the world.

Asko, my calm, my strength, my first day of spring, my husband. I love you like the circle that has no end.